How to Raise Good Children

How to Raise Good Children

Encouraging Moral Growth

LAUREL HUGHES

Abingdon Press / Nashville

HOW TO RAISE GOOD CHILDREN

Copyright © 1988 by Abingdon Press

This book is printed on acid-free paper.

Library of Congress Cataloging-in-Publication Data

HUGHES, LAUREL, 1952–
    How to raise good children.
    Bibliography: p.
    1. Child rearing.   2. Moral development.
3. Children—Conduct of life.   I. Title.
HQ769.H82   1988   649'.7   88-947

ISBN 0-687-17926-2 (alk. paper)

COVER AND BOOK DESIGN BY
JOHN R. ROBINSON

All scripture quotations except where noted are taken from the *Holy Bible:
New International Version.* Copyright © 1973, 1978, 1984 by the International
Bible Society. Used by permission of Zondervan Bible Publishers.

The scripture quotation noted KJV is from the King James Version of the Bible.

Material on pages 58, 74, and 137-38 attributed to Thomas Lickona is from
RAISING GOOD CHILDREN by Dr. Thomas Lickona. Copyright © 1983 by
Thomas Lickona. Reprinted by permission of Bantam Books. All rights reserved.

MANUFACTURED BY THE PARTHENON PRESS AT
Nashville, Tennessee, United States of America

For Bill

Acknowledgments

The following clinicians and professionals provided me with consultation and significantly assisted me as I prepared the content of this book: Cathleen Smith, Ph.D.; Richard Diller, Ph.D.; Lee Doppelt, Ph.D.; and Howard Deitch, Ph.D. I am also grateful for input received from Patricia Fleenor Hall, Ph.D.; Ricks Warren, Ph.D.; and Hank Robb, Ph.D.

I am indebted to many other individuals for their input and moral support as I have put together these materials. Unfortunately, they are too numerous for me to be able to mention them all by name:

the congregation of the Beaverton Free Methodist Church, especially my women's Bible study group (Darlene Birdsall, Jan Hege, Carole Logue, and Pat Van Schoiack);

the gang out at the Oregon Graduate School of Professional Psychology, especially the West-Side Study Group (Doug Anderson, Donna Houston, Dave Montgomery, and Arnie Staite);

my family, especially Bill, Frank, Ben, and Bridie, as they have shown superhuman patience with my career efforts;

and a special thanks to Marjorie Parsons, who convinced me that I should put these ideas into a book.

Contents

PART ONE

ENCOURAGING MORAL GROWTH

Why?

CHAPTER ONE

Introduction

Our children are floundering in a moral morass. Even grade-school children are being forced to make serious decisions about drugs, sex, and their basic integrity at a time of life when earlier generations had worries no greater than not being invited to someone's birthday party. The destructive life-styles of some families expose children to a mockery of interpersonal commitment and responsibility. Television, magazines, and other media flaunt and encourage turning away from moral values.

We as parents are uneasy about the social climate inhabiting our children's world, and rightly so. No matter how much we attempt to shelter our children, we cannot expect to hide unfortunate realities from them forever. Pretending immorality does not exist is hopeless anyway. Who could escape a lion's grasp by denying its glaring anticipation at the foot of the path? Children need guidance and training that prepares them for the inner battle facing them today, and that faces them during their adult futures.

Clear-cut childrearing guidelines are not easy to come by. Although entire walls of bookstores are often devoted to volumes on childrearing psychology, the sheer numbers alone can confuse the consumer. Every author seems to have his or her own idea of which magic formula will result in the best behaved, most psychologically sound child. These various formulas often conflict, even though the authors may have done exceptional jobs of rationalizing them. Trying to dovetail all of the available approaches can be exasperating, if not overwhelming.

Many childrearing manuals, particularly those with a religious orientation, place a heavy emphasis on building children's morals through punishment. After all, the Old Testament makes several references to the use of the rod while disciplining children. Proverbs 22:15 tells us that "folly is bound up in the heart of a child, but the rod of discipline will drive it far from him" (NIV). Unfortunately, parents have beaten their children to death with those very words on their lips. The messages of love, understanding, and kindness found in religious teachings are clearly not consistent with injuring children. However, the popular literal interpretation of the "rod" passages of Scripture has encouraged many parents toward a limited understanding of discipline. Because of this, some well-meaning parents have been drawn into the immoral vacuum of child abuse when their true intention was to correct a child.

Another popular form of discipline to be found sprinkled throughout the childrearing literature is the concept of rewards. Rewards do indeed get children to do what you want them to do. Rewards are also successful in creating desired behaviors in dogs, cats, pigeons, flatworms, and in just about any other critter you would care to mention. However, my personal belief is that there is more to reckon with in human beings than can be found in lower animals. Whether you are coming from the angle of the increased cerebral mass of our brains or from a belief in the existence of a human soul, human beings are qualitatively different. Although rewards may increase certain behaviors, they may not touch or take into account who a child is as a human being. And what kind of message are we giving a child concerning his self-worth and identity if we use the same methods on him as we use on the family pet?

These reward and punishment models of discipline have other drawbacks as well. The central difficulty, as I see it, is that rewards and punishment do not cause children to behave because it is their personal choice. The children behave in order to get a reward or to avoid a punishment. As they say in gangster movies, the child has been "given an offer he can't refuse." This model of discipline does not provide a motivational reason for a child to behave morally at times when no reward or punishment is apparent. The result is that when the child is in such a situation, he will simply do as he sees fit. Because they do not provide an inner personal motivation, I call these types of discipline "coercion models."

Coercion models have the potential to do tremendous damage to a child's moral growth. This potential lies within the method's demand for absolute obedience, with some type of pain being inflicted for any deviations. As a result, the child learns to look to external cues—rather than to his moral beliefs—as a source of guidance. This concept will be discussed in greater detail throughout this book. For now, the following illustrative example serves to point out the extreme outcomes possible as a result of using coercion models.

Alice Miller, a Swiss psychoanalyst, has spent more than twenty years studying the concept of parental demands for obedience.[1] In addition to working with her own patients, she has researched the childhoods of numerous leaders of the Third Reich from the World War II era. Among these leaders, Miller reports that she could not find a single individual who had not had an extremely strict, rigid, moralistic upbringing. As children they were taught to obey unquestioningly. Parents had the absolute, final say over everything. Any show of emotion over parental demands was viewed as rebellion and lack of respect, and resulted in even more disciplinary measures. They learned to turn off their feelings, to ignore what the concepts of right and wrong might be, and to blindly obey the dictates of their parents.

When Hitler came along, these men were ripe for the picking. Hitler took the place of the authoritarian fathers they had lost when they grew up and left home. Not knowing how to seek direction on their own, they willingly accepted it from their Führer. They found no difficulty in carrying out murderous orders because their responsibility was to obey, not to think or question. And obey they did. They had been raised to believe that right and wrong rest solely within the views of the authority figure. The result was the Holocaust.

I would like to interject that I am not arguing against obedience. The basic concept of obedience is both sociologically sound and consistent with most religious teachings. Imagine the chaos we would be living in if nobody obeyed traffic signals! However, the means by which past generations have chosen to teach obedience have wreaked havoc throughout history. My desire is to present options for teaching morals that result in fewer destructive side effects. There *is* a happy medium. Children can learn to obey without your relying on coercion. They find their morals through knowing themselves, not through behaviors forced on them by others. And it is through knowing themselves that they learn to love, and thereby to care about their fellow human beings.

James Dobson suggests that an optimum time for expressing love and affection to a child is right after the child has been spanked.[2] His rationale is that such an approach teaches the child that the punishment was directed at the child's behavior, rather than toward the child himself, and that the child is still lovable. Perhaps. But I would think not. Young children are developmentally unable to deal with abstractions, and without such an ability, I find it hard to believe that they can sort out all of those variables—especially when they are in pain.

Affection after spanking can backfire on so many levels that trying to consider them all boggles the mind. Nevertheless, the following summary provides the gist of my objections:

1. It can reward misbehavior. The child receives love and affection in addition to punishment almost immediately after having misbehaved, which gives the misdeed reward appeal. This is especially true in a home situation where the parents' time and affection are hard to come by. It has been well established that children who receive limited parental attention will purposely misbehave, since a child prefers even negative attention to not receiving any attention at all. Imagine the increased possibility of misbehavior by such a child if the child knows that he will not only receive attention, but affection as well!

2. It teaches the child to ignore his true feelings. After somebody hits us, we do not feel like hugging our attacker. Our true feelings are those of rage and indignation. By insisting on hitting and then hugging a child, we are teaching that child to ignore his feelings in order to go along with what we want. Only through knowing and accepting his own feelings will a child be able to experience empathy for others, and empathy is central to a child's ability to make moral choices in a way that considers the feelings of others. This hit-hug maneuver therefore contributes to the downfall of the most valuable tool the child has for developing a moral sense of right and wrong.

It is true that some children actually show a desire to be hugged after being struck. One reason for this anomaly is that the parent has taught the child to expect it. Another reason is that although the child is justifiably enraged, this feeling isn't anywhere near so disturbing as the feeling of being so seemingly alienated from the parent's affection. He therefore ignores the rage in order to deal with the fear of losing the parent's love. Some children who are extremely sensitive may go to pieces after being spanked, and do need to be comforted. But if the child is that sensitive, I question whether such a severe punishment is actually necessary to get disciplinary results. This type of child might be disciplined just as effectively by something as modest as a stern look from his parent.

3. It teaches a model of masochism. The reward-punishment model is not the only model of learning provided by behavioral research. Another important learning model is called "classical conditioning." This model has shown that when two occurrences are artificially paired, we learn to experience them together long after the original pairing. For example, if we have had a preponderance of frightening experiences with dogs, we will be likely to pair dogs and fear. As a result, when we see a dog, we feel fear. If we happened to be listening to a certain song on the radio just as our spouse proposed marriage, we probably still have nice feelings whenever we hear that song.

Hugging a child after hitting teaches the child to pair violence with love, and this is the classic model for masochism. The profundity of how easily such learning can come about is especially disturbing when we consider the fact that spankings generally occur on children's little bottoms, which results in some genital stimulation, and is then followed by hugs and affection. More graphic elaboration of the potential impact of all this on our children's future sexual functioning and marital relationships is not necessary for us to recognize the dynamite we are toying with when we pair their experience of violence with love.

In light of these drawbacks, why has the hit-hug practice gained such wide acceptance? I tend to believe that parents are eager to hug their children after spanking them because they experience vague feelings of guilt. One of the values our society teaches is that you don't go around hitting people. Furthermore, any parent who is capable of even a modicum of empathy is going to feel bad after hurting another human being. I suspect that the hugging after spanking is less of a need for the child, and more of a need to alleviate the parent's feelings of guilt.

In view of some of the potentially disastrous consequences of this particular combination of love and discipline, it appears that we need to proceed with a little more caution. Love and discipline cannot simply be tossed into the blender, whizzed a few times, then poured out and served. A number of psychologists, psychiatrists, social workers, and other individuals who work with children have devoted their lives to exploring this issue through empirical research. To ignore the fruits of their labors would indeed be a crime against humanity. For this reason we will look at a number of studies from the field of child psychology as we work through this topic.

Before we move on, another clarification is probably in order. Since the coercion model has just been described very negatively, it would be easy to assume that I believe it should be thrown out the window altogether. Nothing could be further from the truth. Direct coercion has its place, but generally as a last resort, rather than as a childrearing mainstay. In chapter 3 we will look in more detail at when to use coercion and when to teach love.

Our children are our nation's most valuable resource: Their moral beliefs are the ones that will guide our nation's future choices. Our job as parents is to equip our children with the tools necessary for building their moral beliefs, and for teaching them to esteem those beliefs more than the beliefs of those around them, which occasionally include even the beliefs of authority figures. I am not supporting indiscriminate revolt and anarchy. Children need to be taught that although they sometimes have to go along with rules they don't endorse, they do have the power to attempt to change the rules. Family life comprises authority figures, a constituency, and rules, and is the ideal testing ground for practicing the negotiation of rules and exploring the reasoning behind them. Obedience and coercion methods will probably always play a role in childrearing as well. But it is only when we stop rigidly clinging to absolute obedience and coercion as our primary modes of discipline that our children will even have a chance to practice putting their morals to use. This book will focus on just how we can help these morals become set in place.

SOME FINAL NOTES

Today the use of pronouns is very difficult for writers. In most places, I have arbitrarily chosen to refer to a singular parent as "she," and a singular child, person, or individual as "he." This strategy ensures that both genders are represented.

Chapters 2, 4, 5, 6, and 8 have exercises at the end, which are intended to help parents learn to use new ideas and techniques. I strongly advise parents to work through the exercises and make use of the sample responses to the exercise questions, which have been provided in the appendix. Reading about a new childrearing method is not enough to change old habits. Through practice you can learn to use new techniques with both confidence and competence.

CHAPTER TWO

Fears

When we try to influence any aspect of our children's development, a number of fears come into play. Fear is one of the most powerful motivators we can have. We deal not only with the physiological reaction of "fright, fight, or flight" substances being pumped into our systems, but also with the cognitive reality of what possible fearful results may occur because of the impending situation.

We have many fears about our children that are well-founded. For example, a child who is inclined to use his fists to solve his disagreements with others will have a difficult interpersonal life as an adult, if that particular pattern proceeds unaltered. A child who frequently steals is bound to have entanglements with the law as an adult if nothing is done to discourage such behavior. We feel distress over the prospect of seeing our children grow up into impoverished emotional lives or suffer the hardships of life in prison. These fears are valid, and can motivate us to seek appropriate ways to try to change our children's behavior.

However, there are other fears that are actually based on conflicts within ourselves. For example, What will the neighbors think? illustrates a conflicted attitude toward discipline. When such a fear motivates us we are likely to use too harsh a punishment, or a punishment visible to or approved of by our neighbors, rather than to intervene in the way that is best for that particular child and situation. Clearly, our purpose for discipline is to shape the behavior of our children, not to shape our neighbors' opinions of us. All too often, however, we do allow these other personal fears or needs to guide our choices. Before we can begin to understand and properly use new intervention techniques, we must understand and come to grips with the fears that may interfere with our judgment.

Concerns over a child's moral development produce their own brand of parental fears, especially for those of us having strong moral and religious convictions. We are much more likely to be upset when our child tells huge obvious lies to our pastor than when our child is a little slow in learning to tie his shoes. Sometimes we see our children's moral deficiencies as a reflection of ourselves and our parenting ability. From this misperception spew many fears that should have little to do with our choices of discipline.

There are probably as many variations of parental fears as there are parents. This chapter attempts to group these fears into several basic categories or ideas. We will look at how each of these fears gets in the way of decision making when we are trying to choose a form of discipline. We will then look for ways to learn about where these fears are really coming from.

"I'M A FAILURE AS A PARENT!"

When a child does not measure up in some area of morality, parents sometimes blame themselves. "If only I'd done this," or "If I hadn't done that" are among the various chastisements we inflict on ourselves. We find all sorts of ways to make unfortunate situations appear to be reflections of our own poor parenting. Emotionally, we find that we are experiencing an overabundance of guilt.

One incident that embarrassed me took place when my son Ben was about seven. He and one of his friends had been playing quietly in our backyard for some time when I got a call from my next-door neighbor. Apparently the boys had discovered my bumper crop of cherry tomatoes. Upon finding that the tomatoes were too ripe for eating, they had begun using our neighbors' hot tub for target practice.

A number of different self-blame statements began to race through my mind:

"I knew I shouldn't have let Ben play with that kid! He's always encouraging him to get into some sort of mischief."

"I should have been out there watching those two so I could have headed this thing off at the pass."

"Here I am with all of this advanced training in psychology and I can't even keep my child from doing something as obviously wrong as this."

"If I weren't such a crummy mother, my kids would certainly have turned out better."

When we have these sorts of thoughts and make these sorts of assumptions, we are concluding that the sum of our child's make-up is determined by our own influences. This way of thinking is grandiose. There are many other influences besides parenting style that affect a child's future behavior. The culture our child grows up in provides various norms for behavior. The children at school and playmates in the neighborhood all affect which behaviors are seen as being possible choices for action. Anyone who has had more than one child has recognized how quickly each child's distinct personality emerges, different from that of his siblings. Thus it appears that some of our characteristics are implanted before we are even born. In addition, we cannot forget that our child comes equipped with a capacity to choose what to do or not to do or believe in any given circumstance. Considering these additional influences on our children's choices of behavior, we have no right to take complete responsibility for it.

We as parents are the most important source of guidance our children have, which is why it is imperative that we take our job seriously. However, when we view ourselves as the only relevant factor in our child's behavior it is time for us to step back and assess our relationship with our child. Do we really view our child as an individual, or just as an extension of ourselves?

In reality, children are separate human beings who exhibit their own human foibles just as adults do. Likewise, children need to learn from their mistakes as adults learn from theirs. They need to be approached at such times with an attitude of supportiveness and guidance, rather than be faced with an enraged, self-critical parent who harshly punishes the child as a substitute for the parent's inner desire to punish herself for her own fantasized shortcomings. In addition, as long as a child is encouraged to believe he is merely an appendage of his parents' will, there is no reason for the child to take responsibility for his own actions. If parents appear more than willing to accept the blame themselves, why should the child?

Jerry Schmidt describes a process for dealing with these sorts of parental thoughts and attitudes.[1] He uses a method called "countering." When we have self-defeating thoughts, which are not getting us anywhere, we can answer our own thoughts in a way that brings us back to reality. Here is how I countered my destructive thoughts during the tomato-throwing incident:

1. *I knew I shouldn't have let him play with that kid!* There is no way I could have known that teaming those two would have resulted in tomatoes all over my neighbors' hot tub. In fact, I have no way of knowing that the other kid had anything to do with influencing Ben. It could be something that Ben would have tried somewhere along the line no matter whom he was with.

2. *I should have been out there watching them.* There is no way I can constantly keep track of everything all three of my children do. It is physically impossible. If I tried, I'd go bananas.

3. *I can't even prevent these things by becoming a psychologist.* Sure I have a lot of advanced training. So what? Having knowledge is not the same as being skilled in applying that knowledge. I may have the knowledge of what is necessary for disciplining children, and be skilled at passing along that knowledge to others. However, there are many people who have a greater ability than I in applying this knowledge while childrearing. And that's O.K.!

4. *If I weren't such a crummy mother, my kids would have turned out better.* Baloney. Inherited tendencies, cultural variables, peer influences, and growing independent choices all affect how my kids turn out. My parenting is important, but it's not the only important influence. Besides, this is only one isolated incident. Actually Ben is a pretty neat kid!

Cutting the emotional umbilical cord is an important part of being able to parent rationally. This does not mean that we should discontinue empathizing with our children as they experience the delights and sorrows of daily living. It means we must recognize that our children are unique, separate individuals with God-given characteristics different from our own. Although we may feel for our children, we must realize that our children's life experiences and life choices are separate from ours, and recognize that the ultimate responsibility for their behavior lies within them, not us.

"IT'S NOT FAIR!"

A parent can do everything according to the books and still see her child grow into an adult who at times gives the appearance of being morally bankrupt, an outcome expressed well in a song from the musical *The Fantasticks:* "Plant a radish, get a radish, never any doubt," but with children, "as soon as you think you know what kind you've got, it's what they're not."[2] When we put so much effort into influencing our children's lives, it is only natural that we should look forward to the reward of sending a "perfect person" off into the world on his eighteenth birthday. Unfortunately, this form of justice does not occur so often as we would like. As a result, many of us feel cheated when our children do not turn out as we had anticipated.

The fear buried beneath this state of affairs is loss of control. We have a tremendous emotional investment in our children's futures. We will not stop feeling joy over our children's triumphs and pain over our children's failures just because they have left the roost. In order to protect ourselves against future pain, we pour much time and effort into child discipline, almost as a type of insurance policy. When the insurance does not pay off, that assumed piece of control we so desired is exposed as the invalid assumption that it is, and we feel betrayed.

When we find ourselves in this situation, it can be helpful to examine what role the issue of control plays in our lives. Are our demands to influence our world realistic? Unrealistic attempts to exert control are often a sign of insecurity. A person who is preoccupied with protection against all real or imagined possibilities of unpleasantness, pain, or criticism can become compelled to overcontrol all the factors in her environment that could be possible sources of such discomfort, including her children. The person feels more vulnerable than her environment warrants, and does not believe she has the inner resources to defend herself against painful life situations. Self-image and self-esteem are central issues here.

Many books, both secular and religious, have been written on these subjects. If we discover that our fearful self-concepts are leading to attempts to overcontrol our children, such books can be helpful. We can survive our children's failures! Even if studying self-esteem does not help a parent improve her self-image, just being aware that she isn't placing enough worth on herself can help prevent her low self-worth from influencing how she deals with her children. She can ask herself at the time of her decisions, Am I doing this to protect myself, or because it is the best way to influence my child in a way that *he* needs? As a result, she can make a more rational choice.

"WHAT WILL MY MOTHER [PASTOR, FRIENDS] THINK?"

When our children misbehave, it can be very embarrassing for us. This is particularly true concerning moral behavior. However, while embarrassment or shame can be extremely uncomfortable, it should not be the ruling factor in deciding how to discipline children.

Human beings need closeness with others, and part of feeling close to another person is believing that he accepts you or approves of you. It is not unusual for us to try to protect that approval-acceptance from outside threats. Unfortunately, some people depend too heavily on others' opinions of them. Their need to be approved of is so great that other variables, such as using appropriate measures in disciplining a child, may take second place in order to protect that approval.

When we suspect that this may be happening to us, perhaps it is time to examine whether or not *we* approve of ourselves. If the desire to win the approval of others is responsible for how we run our lives, we may want to look at whether our needs for affection are currently feeling met. One way of deciding this may be to ask ourselves, Is my need to be loved by this person (mother, pastor, friend—whoever it is we are trying to impress with our child discipline) interfering with my judgment about what is right to do?

If the answer is yes, we may need to seek ways to set aside such feelings when making disciplinary decisions. It could be that we will discover that those who truly care about us will continue to do so even if they do not necessarily endorse our childrearing techniques. In addition, we may find that those who act alienated when we do not conform to their disciplinary demands or expectations are not acting in our best interests; and we may even discover that we had been viewed by them more as a pawn for manipulating, and over whom to exert their own self-perceived authority. In other words, love is defined by how people treat one another, not by whether they agree with one another. People whose differences cannot be resolved can "agree to disagree" and continue their friendship from there. If a person risks losing affection because of disagreement, true affection was probably limited to begin with.

Overreliance on the approval of others can also be a symptom of lack of self-confidence in one's own ability to assess the world and make decisions accordingly. My firm belief is that no psychological concept is so difficult that it cannot be explained to the busboy at Harry's Bar and Grill. No slur against busboys is intended here; the point is that people with any amount of education, short of those with extreme mental defect, are capable of learning and correctly using appropriate childrearing techniques. What is essential is not some innate brilliance within the parent; it is the willingness of the parent to educate herself, looking to the available authorities, experts, and research, and then having the self-confidence to act according to her informed judgment.

If we find ourselves questioning our confidence in our parenting or overrelying on the opinions of those around us, we can ask, Why have I chosen to do what I am doing? Are there experts or bodies of research that support my choice? Has it been the experience of many others that this can work? Has it worked when I have tried it in the past? If we can answer these questions satisfactorily, the soundness of our judgment is clear. It shows support for our parenting choices that cannot be denied.

"I'M BEING PUNISHED [OR DESERTED] BY GOD"

Some parents believe that their children's shortcomings, as well as any other affliction in their lives, are the result of some sin of their own for which God is punishing them. This is a very self-centered way of looking at the world. It suggests that God arranges everyone else's lives to center on one individual, namely, the afflicted parent. This does not sound like the fair and loving God described by most religious teachings.

When parents adopt such a view, it generally reflects *their* feelings about themselves, rather than God's feelings about them. This sort of person is so overly self-critical that she continually finds "sin" in her life that "deserves" to be punished, and she assumes that God has the same feelings that she does. Typically she has been sharply and probably unfairly criticized by others during her lifetime. Valuable questions for her to ask would be, What uncomfortable feelings about myself of my own do I attribute to God? and, Where are these feelings *really* coming from? Once we understand the basis of our feelings, we can separate them from both our perception of God and our perception of ourselves. Seeking the aid of a competent psychotherapist or counselor can help us find many answers to these questions.

Matthew 28:20b tells us "And surely I am with you always, to the very end of the age" (NIV). This does not sound like the message of an overpunitive god who judges, condemns, and deserts parents on the basis of their children's behavior. In childrearing we must seek valid information and make sober judgments, but even so we will not necessarily be perfect parents, or turn out a perfect product.

CONCLUSION

This chapter illustrates how our feelings can interfere with doing what is best for our children's moral development. Problems such as lack of self-confidence, an overcritical attitude, insecurity, and even overextended apron strings can all result in using childrearing techniques that are based on our own shortcomings, rather than the needs of our children. All of us experience these feelings to some degree. The intent of exposing them here is to "shake up" our mind-sets, so that our feelings can be viewed in light of whatever detrimental, prejudicial effect they may be having. Once this has been accomplished, we are freer to approach childrearing with an attitude centering more on what works and less on the biases of our emotions.

EXERCISES

Recall a recent incident in which you believe you administered a punishment that was too harsh, too lenient, or in some other way inappropriate or inadequate. Write it out in detail, and respond to the following questions:

1. What fear or fears did you feel at the time of discipline? what pressure or pressures?
2. How did the fear or fears affect your choice of discipline?
3. Why do you believe your choice of discipline was not the best for that situation?
4. What do you think would have been a better choice?
5. The next time you feel that a fear or pressure is influencing you, what will you tell yourself about it in order to reduce the effect it has on you?

Below are some automatic thoughts we may have from time to time. Write statements that counter these thoughts.[3] (See pages 134-35 for examples.)

1. "My children must always love me or I will be miserable."
2. "Making a childrearing mistake is terrible."
3. "My own childhood experience must always affect my parenting."
4. "Every childrearing problem has a perfect solution."
5. "Healthy parents don't get upset with their children."
6. "I must never show any weakness in front of my children."

CHAPTER THREE

Internalization

While children are still in their formative years, parents play the major role in controlling and guiding their lives. As parents we apply many constraints. We tell children when to eat, sleep, bathe, go to school, go to church, do homework, do chores, and when they are free to do as they please. In addition, we provide disciplinary constraints. Inappropriate behaviors are met with all sorts of consequences, such as loss of privileges, additional chores, lectures, confinement to the home, and corporal punishment. We encourage desired behaviors through praise and various other rewards.

All of these controls placed on the child are external. They encourage the child to look outside himself to decide what he is going to do. Actually, this is the main reason we provide our children with restraints. The purpose of using reward and punishment is to increase the likelihood that our child will behave in a way that avoids his being punished or that may result in a reward. As long as a child is too immature or unknowledgeable to make adequate choices using his own judgment, this type of discipline is extremely valuable.

However, children eventually grow into adults. As adults they will use their own judgment in decision making, and will need a moral structure on which to base their judgment. As we discussed earlier, a strict reward-and-punishment model of discipline does not provide a moral structure because it trains the child to look *outside* himself to decide what is right or wrong. Making use of a moral structure involves looking *inside* ourselves to decide what is right or wrong. The focus of encouraging the development of inner personal values is therefore completely opposite from the fruits of a reward-and-punishment orientation.

We all know people who have not progressed past looking outside themselves for direction. The following attitudes illustrate how they reason:

"We make illegal deductions on our income tax. But it's O.K.; everybody does it."

"It's all right to sneak into the show without buying a ticket, as long as you don't get caught."

"My friends will really be impressed with me if I can drink them under the table."

"Messing around is O.K. as long as your spouse doesn't find out."

As we can see, these people base how they behave on values adhered to by others or consequences received from others. An inner belief system of right and wrong does not enter into their decisions because they have been trained to look to external consequences for direction.

Considering all of the garbage there is in this world for our children to observe, we can understand why their having an external basis for deciding what to do is a scary prospect for us as parents. Preventing this external focus can be facilitated by using disciplinary measures that emphasize focusing on a moral structure within the child himself. As children grow older we can gently wean them from our control and guide them toward activating their own moral beliefs; beliefs we can instill and strengthen throughout their childhood. When a person leaves childhood and enters adulthood, he needs to have a firmly established idea of right and wrong to cling to at times of indecision, rather than be left to flounder and grasp at any convenient life raft that happens to drift by.

At first glance this appears to be a tall order. Almost all traditional disciplinary methods employ external consequences, rather than strengthening inner focus and convictions. Fortunately, a relatively new area of investigation in the field of child development focuses on the internal self. It is a part of social learning theory known as the study of prosocial behavior. As the name suggests, it is a study of how children internalize the values acceptable to their society and those who raise them. We will be looking at recent research in the area of prosocial behavior, and will explore ways of using this research to teach our children moral behavior.

THE ROLE OF PRINCIPLED THINKING

It is so easy to get caught up in legalism. Do's and don'ts are solid and dependable. There is little room for uncertainty when an exact behavior for a specific circumstance is called for. We find security in absolutes because within them we know whether what we are doing is right or wrong.

Unfortunately, real-world applications of rules are not always so clear-cut. For example, the concept of being nice to others is generally a good rule to follow. If we always endeavor to be kind and considerate toward others, most of the time interpersonal situations will work out for the best. However, there are times when such an approach will backfire. This is particularly true when we have to say no to others' requests, just because we will be unreasonably inconvenienced or overextended if we say yes. If we went along with the rule of being considerate of others' feelings, to the exclusion of protecting our own needs, we would end up so burnt out, frustrated, and angry with others that nobody's best interests would be served.

Another example is confrontation. Having to tell people that they are doing something offensive or somehow harmful to us or others is not pleasant for either party. If all we ever did was look the other way when people behaved aggressively and unfairly, we would certainly be following the rule of being considerate of the aggressor. But what about the feelings of the victims? By not confronting the aggressor, we would not be considering those who must suffer because of the aggressor's actions. In this case, we end up with a double bind, because we cannot follow the rule concerning either party without simultaneously breaking the rule.

Living by absolute rules does not work because behavioral rules are concrete. They describe a specific way of behaving. And a rule cannot address every possible situation to which the behavior can be applied. There are too many possibilities for a behavioral rule to be all inclusive. The result is that the behavior may not fit every given situation.

Because of these shortcomings, we need to look beyond absolute rules and go back to where we found them. Rules are based on *principles*. These principles are abstractions, but they come closer to being the absolutes we live by and the goals we aim toward. Rules are merely the basic guidelines we construct out of convenience as a means of applying our principles.

The rule of trying to be kind and considerate requires placing a high priority on the underlying principle of love, or caring about our fellow human beings. Most of the time, if we are kind and considerate toward others, we will be serving this principle of caring. This is why making rules is so useful. But if the rule does not serve the principle, we should be flexible enough to disregard the rule for the sake of acting on our principles.

If we apply the abstract principle of caring about others to the preceding examples, rather than the absolute rule of being kind no matter what, the outcomes do not seem so counterproductive. We can say no to another's unreasonable request because we know that if we say yes, our resulting resentment will eventually impair the relationship, and impairing relationships is not a caring thing to do. Besides, caring about ourselves and our own needs is the only way we can protect and nurture the resources we have to offer others. Confrontation becomes more simplified because a caring philosophy backs actions that will serve and protect the needs and rights of many, as opposed to protecting the desires of one.

Clearly, being aware of our moral principles is a necessity for making moral choices. Researchers in the area of child development, most notably Lawrence Kohlberg,[1] have found that the ability to make moral choices generally passes through six developmental stages. Each of these stages illustrates a different way of deciding what would be the right thing to do. Kohlberg organized the stages as a hierarchy, through which children are thought to progress; it is assumed that the principle of justice is the highest moral principle. Following is a summary of these stages:

Stage 1: . . . The physical consequences of an action determine whether it is good or bad. Avoiding punishment and bowing to superior power are valued positively.

Stage 2: . . . Right action consists of behavior that satisfies one's own needs. Human relations are viewed in marketplace terms. Reciprocity occurs, but is seen in a pragmatic way, i.e., "you scratch my back and I'll scratch yours."

Stage 3: . . . Good behaviors are those that please or are approved by others. There is much emphasis on conformity and being "nice."

Stage 4: . . . Focus is on authority or rules. It is right to do one's duty, show respect for authority, and maintain the social order.

Stage 5: . . . This stage has a utilitarian, legalistic tone. Correct behavior is defined in terms of standards agreed upon by society. Awareness of the relativism of personal values and the need for consensus is important.

Stage 6: . . . Morality is defined as a decision of conscience. Ethical principles are self-chosen, based on abstract concepts (e.g., the Golden Rule) rather than concrete rules (e.g., the Ten Commandments).[2]

One of the most striking pertinent characteristics of this hierarchy is where the punishment and obedience orientation falls. It is seen as the most primitive, childish means of moral reasoning a person can use. Yet this is what the coercion method of childrearing teaches! What is even more striking is that the stage theorists camp on the opposite side of the river from the social learning theorists, occasionally even directing intellectual crossfire toward one another. Yet there is substantial agreement between the two camps concerning the undesirability of a punishment-and-obedience orientation.

Likewise, notice the parallel in moving from an external focus to an internal focus. Early stages tend to look for external consequences as a guide for actions, and answer the question, What's in it for me? Later stages involve inner direction, which places greater emphasis on the question, What protects the feelings and rights of all?

This progression also parallels the moral progression found as we move from the Old Testament to the New Testament. Leviticus and Deuteronomy are loaded with various rules and regulations, and the most famous set of rules of all time—the Ten Commandments—can also be found in the Old Testament. But when Jesus enters the scene in the New Testament, he acts out a message of "hey, wait a minute!" as he reacts to others' interpretations of Old Testament rules. He repeatedly criticizes the Pharisees for their fanatical adherence to rules. Rather than condoning the stoning of an adulterous woman, he advises the mob that "if any one of you is without sin, let him be the first to throw a stone at her" (John 8:7b NIV), which leads to the prescribed consequence for adultery not being followed. He performs healings and pursues other activities on the Sabbath, even though a commandment specifically instructs us to keep that day holy.

Jesus' most likely explanation for his seeming disregard for Old Testament rules can be found in Mark 12:29-31:

> "The most important [commandment]," answers Jesus, is this: ". . . Love the Lord your God with all your heart and with all your soul and with all your mind and with all your strength." The second is this: "Love your neighbor as yourself." There is no commandment greater than these. (NIV)

What he is both teaching and modeling is that rules in and of themselves are not our most important concern. The principle of loving God, your neighbor, and yourself—from which Old Testament rules and moral issues flow—is what takes priority over any individual rule. Another way of looking at it is that God's principles are the absolutes; the rules are only examples of ways his principles may be played out, and are therefore not absolute.

With these concepts as a backdrop, we will next look at the principle of caring about others, and how it appears in a child's behavior.

ALTRUISM

Caring about fellow human beings is studied in the scientific world under the label "altruism." Altruism involves acts where there is no apparent external reward for the doer. For example, a child who picks up his toys because his mother promises to take him to the zoo if he does so is not being altruistic. If he picks up his toys because he knows his mother will be pleased with him, he is still not being altruistic, because he is only following through in order to get a pat on the head from mom. To be truly altruistic, the child would have to pick up his toys because he knows it would make his mother happy, whether she knows he did it or not.

There are many different types of altruistic acts, but they all have that same characteristic of selflessness or self-sacrifice. A list of these acts would include giving, helping, sharing, cooperating, making restitution, defending, protecting, comforting, encouraging, and showing concern, consideration, or affection for others.[3]

A prerequisite for altruism is a capacity for *empathy*. Having empathic ability means that a person can recognize, understand, and react to the feelings of others. For example, if a child sees his friend fall down and skin his knee, he will feel bad for that friend even though he has not been injured himself. If he sees one child taking unfair advantage of another, he will feel the same rage as does the victimized child. Empathy allows a child to have almost as much fun watching another child open his birthday presents as when the presents are his own. Empathy is an indispensable ingredient of altruism. Before a child can act in a way that considers others, he must first be sensitive to their emotions and be able to understand how his actions can affect them.

Very young children appear to be able to recognize emotional reactions. Studies of two-day-old infants have shown that newborns respond more strongly to the sound of other infants crying than to other noises of equivalent pitch and volume.[4] Anyone who has had nursery duty of some sort can attest to this fact: If one baby starts crying, at least one other is likely to join in. Therefore, recognizing the feelings of others is not something that we have to instill in our children. It is a normal, inborn tendency. This should be no surprise to parents of a religious persuasion, since religion recognizes the existence of an inner spiritual self in all human beings as a result of their being created in the image of a loving God. Our job is to use forms of discipline that will encourage and strengthen our children's natural precursors of empathy.

HOW DOES EMPATHY AFFECT MORALITY?

The question burning in most of our minds is whether our childrearing practices will encourage our children to make wise, socially acceptable choices for their lives. We will explore the rationale for the choice of focusing on empathy as the key to moral behavior.

People who care about other people weigh their actions more carefully than those who do not care about what happens to others. Empathy causes a person to avoid doing something that will hurt another because he knows that if he does, he will also hurt. Likewise, empathy influences a person toward being more willing to do reasonable special favors for others, since he will feel a pleasure similar to that experienced by the recipient of the act.

The person incapable of empathy, sometimes clinically termed *sociopathic,* is not encumbered with such guidelines. He feels pain or pleasure only in relation to what affects him personally. Therefore, he makes his choices according to what's in it for him. Sociopaths frequently climb business ladders quickly, since they have no concern for who they have to step on to get to where they want to go. But as could be expected, their interpersonal lives are generally a shambles. Since their moral choices involve only what feels good to them personally or furthers their own interests, few significant others are willing to hang around indefinitely to have their rights and feelings stomped on.

Most moral standards involve consideration for the feelings and rights of others. Stealing is morally unacceptable because it does not respect others' rights of ownership. Profane language offends others. Charity helps others. Obeying a democracy's laws respects the choice of the majority of others. Lying misleads others. All of these acts are involved with morality because they consider the rights and feelings of all, rather than restrict themselves to the selfish desires of one. An ability to be concerned for others is therefore an absolute necessity for making moral choices at the higher levels of Kohlberg's hierarchy.

An empathic person will avoid promiscuity. He may at first be tempted by the promise of immediate pleasure. However, he considers how such behavior could spread various diseases to others. He realizes that such behavior could take advantage of others emotionally. He recognizes the possibility of creating unwanted, unhappy children, who could in turn contribute to the misery of many. An empathic person will not drink and drive. He knows that drinking impairs his judgment, and understands that a car is a lethal weapon when not under complete control. He will not risk injuring others because he can imagine the experience of an injured person. An empathic person will think twice about becoming involved with illegal drugs. He is aware of how drug use alienates him in his relationships with those around him and can recognize the pain he would be causing. In addition, he will avoid fostering an industry so brutal toward others in its daily dealings, since he cares about the well-being of others. An empathic person will not cheat others out of what is rightfully theirs because he knows how being cheated must feel. An empathic person will be willing to help a person he sees in distress because he is aware of how it must feel to need help and receive it. An empathic person will defend the rights of another because he recognizes what it feels like to be taken advantage of. An empathic person will use tact when dealing with sensitive issues in order to cushion the feelings of others because he would feel guilty over causing them unnecessary pain. An empathic person would rather share his possessions than watch someone do without because he can experience that person's feelings of need.

In summary, an empathic person will choose morality over immorality because it is based on caring about other human beings and because he can feel the experience of those who are subjected to others' immoral choices.

MORAL VERSUS COERCIVE INTERVENTIONS

In order to help children develop their internal moral structure, two areas of learning emerge as the central goals. Interventions that assist children by teaching the moral principle of caring about people and helping them retain and understand their empathic feelings are what I call *moral interventions*. Childrearing methods that are rooted in coercion, mainly reward and punishment, I will refer to as *coercive interventions*.

I advise you not to expect instant results from moral interventions. We saw in our discussion of empathy and altruism that developing internal values takes time. The child learns gradually how he experiences his feelings toward others, and over time learns to make choices that seem morally correct. This is one of the difficult parts of childrearing. When parents are using a correct intervention they want the immediate feedback of a visibly changed child. This is in part so that they can know they are doing the right thing, and partly so that they can pat themselves on the back for a job well done. Unfortunately, this is not always possible with internal change, since a child's internal state of mind is not directly observable. We can only guess, by looking at their behavior, which way their little wheels are turning, and the type of situation in which we intervene may not come up again for days or even months. This is not as immediately gratifying as is a child instantly shutting a forbidden drawer after being swatted or yelled at. Sometimes we need to muster extra tolerance for delay of gratification just to preserve our confidence in ourselves as parents!

Knowing just how to intervene involves deciding the most compelling factor or lesson to be learned from a situation. Is it more important that the child immediately stop what he is doing? Or is it a situation in which a moral intervention would be wise? For example, if a child has just shoplifted a one-thousand-dollar bracelet or is about to run out into the street in front of a car, telling him how his actions affect others is not going to be enough. Without immediate restitution, the stealing child may experience legal consequences. And without quick preventive measures such as yelling or physical restraint, the child running into the street could suffer grave injury. In these situations, controlling the child's immediate behavior is more important than a moral lesson. Moral virtues can always be expounded after the emergency has passed.

However, if a child refuses to help another child find his coat, no grave consequences will take place because of his noncompliance with the rules of helpful behavior. In this case, we could use a moral intervention, such as explaining how his refusal to help makes the other child feel. He may still refuse to help, but the contact made with his empathic ability will increase the likelihood that he will spontaneously help the next time such a situation arises. On the other hand, an impatient parent may scold or punish the child for his nonaltruistic behavior. Under these circumstances, the child loses an opportunity to get in touch with his empathic ability. He will probably also be likely to resent the child who needed help, which may actually inhibit empathic growth.

We can sometimes decide which type of intervention to use by considering whether the behavior is owing to basic immaturity. For example, it is fairly normal for a six-year-old boy to want to pound his younger sister from time to time. By the time he becomes a twenty-one-year-old man, this tendency normally will have worn off, since he pursues more mature interests and challenges. Since immature attitudes toward siblings are naturally grown out of, short-term methods of controlling behavior are adequate. Moral exhortations could have some effect on such children's future empathic ability, but meanwhile the younger sisters of the world would be perpetually black-and-blue.

The coercive-versus-moral interventions dilemma can also be looked at by way of short-term versus long-term results. Reward and punishment provide short-term results. They control the immediate situation, and the effects tend to wear off after the consequences cease. They are sufficient for the needs of school settings and other short-term, structured programs. Moral interventions may or may not have an immediate effect on the child's behavior. However, moral interventions have a long-term cumulative effect in determining how the child will react in the future.

There are other unfortunate circumstances where we must resort to coercion methods. These situations arise when the child has stopped listening to his parents. When parents are too demanding and controlling, children may give up trying to meet their impossible demands and do as they see fit. If parents are inconsistent or hypocritical in their discipline, the child loses respect for their belief systems, and gives up on trying to make any sense out of them. When children are completely undisciplined and left to form beliefs on their own, they learn to function on an emotional survival level, and become uninterested in any pearls of wisdom from parents who have up until then seemed like a dry well.

Consistent application of reasonable reward-and-punishment contingencies can make a big difference for this sort of child. The parent would finally be establishing firm, realistic boundaries, which provide both security and trust. Furthermore, the extreme misbehavior (which is usually found in children who have given up on parents) has been put under some control. Once trust is established and behaviors are controlled, parents can move on to encouraging higher moral functioning. Essentially, the task mirrors the hierarchy of moral reasoning: teaching the child to respect punishment and obedience as a beginning point, and then moving on to more sophisticated parenting.

In summary, deciding whether to use coercive interventions or moral interventions involves the following questions:

1. What will be the consequences if I do nothing?
2. Will this behavior dissipate with age?
3. Am I being tuned out to the point where I need to use coercion just to catch his attention?
4. Am I using enough moral interventions to counterbalance the possible destructive side effects of coercion?

CONCLUSION

As we look at children's natural tendency toward empathy, and how it can be enhanced or buried, a sad commentary on Western childrearing emerges. Have you ever noticed how easily children can make friends? Even language is not a barrier. Children communicate with one another in ways that transcend adult reason and convention. They share a common, understood, carefree, and fun-loving attitude, which is not encumbered by adult modes of interpersonal behavior. Yet this wonderful, natural, empathic sensing ability tends to be lost as children undergo socialization.

Do adult realities really necessitate the extinguishing of empathy? I can't help but wonder. What if we didn't destroy empathy during childrearing? What if our culture did spend less time coercing children away from their feelings, and instead built up this natural empathy through moral interventions?

This would be the grand experiment. And this is one experiment that is not controlled by scientists. The power is ours as parents, and can be exercised through the methods of discipline we choose.

PART Two

ENCOURAGING MORAL GROWTH

How?

CHAPTER FOUR

What to Do After Your Child Does Something Good

Occasionally our children may delight us by performing a kindness, such as sharing candy with another child, without being prompted. Being on the alert for such voluntary acts of altruism is crucial. Some of the most effective things we can do involve our reactions to spontaneous good behavior. This chapter will look at three: positive reinforcement, inner labeling, and accepting offers of altruism.

POSITIVE REINFORCEMENT

Positive reinforcement is a well-known reward system. One popular example uses the aid of a device known as a Skinner box, named for the founder of the theory of operant conditioning, B. F. Skinner. The box is a completely enclosed structure equipped with a bar-pressing or other device an animal can manipulate. When the animal activates the device, it receives the reward of food. Once the animal learns that pressing the bar results in the reward of food, it will continue to press the bar indefinitely (as long as it is hungry!).

However, the experimenter may decide that he no longer wants the animal to press the bar. When this is the case, he will stop allowing food to drop into the box when the animal presses the bar. Once the animal discovers that it will no longer receive the reward, it will press the bar less and less, eventually stopping altogether. This process is called *extinction*. Much of what this example shows about extinction is common sense. When we get hungry and go to the refrigerator to find a snack, we do not return to the refrigerator a number of times if every time we open it we find it empty. Most likely we forget about the refrigerator and try the cupboards, go to the store, or send out for pizza instead. In this case, the behavior of refrigerator-door opening is extinguished, since it no longer results in the reward of snacks.

Many childrearing manuals put a heavy emphasis on the use of rewards to get children to cooperate. As long as rewards keep flowing after the child performs the desired behaviors, those behaviors will indeed continue to be performed. For young children whose immaturity prevents them from behaving appropriately on the basis of their own judgment, rewards are a valuable tool in manipulating their actions. However, unless *internalization* has taken place (we will return to this concept), once the parent stops rewarding the desired behavior—out of forgetfulness, or because the child has grown up and left home—the desired behavior will no longer occur.

One common example of rewards and extinction concerns paying children to perform certain tasks. A mother decides that she would like her child to clear the table after dinner, and offers to pay him a quarter every time he does it. The child tries clearing the table, and his mother gives him a quarter. He decides that maybe there is something for him in this venture after all. As long as he continues receiving quarters for services rendered, he continues to clear the table. However, after a while the mother decides that the system has become too costly. She would prefer that it become one of the child's responsibilities, rather than a favor to Mom, so she discontinues the quarters. When the child discovers that he will no longer receive his incentive for clearing the table, he eventually stops clearing it. The desired behavior is extinguished because it no longer results in a reward.

However, he might have continued clearing the table if some *internal* basis for continuing the behavior had been nurtured. In other words, all on his own he might have developed a self-reward system, and would continue to reward himself after the external reward from his mother had ceased. He might or might not be consciously aware of these rewards. Here are some examples:

"I feel grown up and responsible when I do this by myself every day."

"It makes me feel good when I see some of the load taken off Mom."

"I feel like a helpful person when I clear the table. I like discovering that about myself."

Giving himself any of these internal messages might encourage him to continue clearing the table even though he was no longer receiving a quarter. He would feel internally rewarded during helpful behavior, and thus the helpful behavior would continue to take place. Unfortunately, as in this case, internal reward systems do not usually take over after an external one has been used. When an external reward system is used, the child focuses on looking for consequences from the outside to decide his behavior. Unless an internal reinforcer is extremely powerful within a child, he will not even notice its presence, since he has been enticed to look outside himself for guidance of his behavior.

As might be expected, psychologists have examined positive reinforcement by how well it promotes moral growth. Numerous studies have suggested that giving either material rewards such as money or candy, and social rewards such as praise, will increase the likelihood of a child's practicing altruistic habits. However, these studies do not look at the rate of helpful behavior after the rewards have stopped. As with any other form of positive reinforcement, we would expect the helpful behavior to also stop when it no longer results in a reward.

One study attempted to sort out the effects of rewards by following seven-year-olds' and eight-year-olds' sharing with telling them, "That was a fine thing you did" (a social reward), or with giving them a penny (a material reward).[1] When asked later why they had shared, the socially rewarded children said they had shared because of a concern for the welfare of the other child. The materially rewarded children said they had shared in order to get a penny. These results are consistent with the idea that material rewards actually encourage a self-oriented, external focus. In view of this study, it appears that rewards do not provide the route to encouraging the internalized focus necessary for moral behavior. Rewards can even have a negative effect. Several studies indicate that if a child begins receiving material rewards for a behavior he was already frequently performing on his own, the behavior will actually *decrease* from the original rate after the material reward is removed.[2] This seems to be a clear example of how teaching a child to look outside himself for consequences draws him away from his own inner values. Introducing a material reward system actually works against moral development having already taken place.

On the other hand, the social reward appears to have helped the children find their empathic ability. Why does this happen? One explanation is that telling a child that an act of his was good implies to him that there is a basic value system of good and bad. Although this is not yet actual internalization, social rewards appear to suggest to the child that he can be compelled by his own inner values. This is a prerequisite for internalizing and using a value system.

INNER LABELING

One of the outstanding characteristics of Jesus, one of the greatest moral teachers, was his ability to see the good in everybody. He came across a variety of people who could easily have been chastised for their errant life-styles. Yet in only a small minority of incidences does the New Testament report Jesus as admonishing people. Instead, he looked to that part of the person capable of love and obedience and sought to confront the person there. The woman at the well, the adulteress, and even an afflicted man trying to reach a healing pool were all ministered to by his "Go, and sin no more" description of their inner capacities. He did not go into an outward derogatory description and punishment of the errors in their past behavior. He knew they were capable of a more highly developed moral life-style and pointed out to them that precious ability.

In addition to universal human capabilities, Jesus recognized individual gifts within various persons. Some of his disciples were even renamed in a manner that pointed out their inner gifts as they worked within the disciples' ministries: Peter "the Rock" and Barnabas "the Encourager." Such labels told the disciples who they were and gave them confidence in their ability to carry out God's plans for their lives. Even as Moses asked God what his name was, a meaningless outward title was not entertained. God stated simply that he is "I am," a state of inner being, not a product of outward behaviors.

Research has shown that children will behave in a way that is the same as the inner labels placed on them. If a child is told he is a responsible person after he has acted responsibly, he will be more likely to behave responsibly in the future than a child who is not given such a label. For example, if Johnny shares his candy with Suzie, a parent can say, "You must be one of those nice, generous persons who care about other people's feelings." Or if Mary helps Tommy fix his bike, a parent could say, "Mary, you sure are a nice helpful person." These sorts of statements have been found to greatly increase sharing and helping. The positive effect of labeling children's inner selves has been shown to influence many other characteristics, such as patience,[3] cooperativeness,[4] and feeling guilt over transgression.[5]

Another form of inner labeling involves pointing out to a child what his feelings are like when he does something nice. For example, if a child cleans up a mess without any outside encouragement, a parent can say, "Wow, you must feel really good inside about being such a good helper" or "I'll bet you get nice feelings inside when you do things like that for people." Children learn from this type of response that their feelings are natural and acceptable, and it allows them to enjoy experiencing their feelings as well. Getting in touch with one's feelings is the first step toward developing empathy. Fortunate is the child who has parents who accept and support feelings!

Children are not always sure why they have chosen to share or cooperate. Possibly they have seen someone they admire act in this way, or perhaps their empathy is catching up with them. In either case, a state of ambiguity exists in the child's mind. He will accept whatever explanation for his behavior the parent suggests. This is a tremendous opportunity for parents to effectively point out to children their inner empathic selves, and is one reason inner labeling is so successful.

Inner labeling has been found to be even more effective than social rewards. In one study children who performed acts of altruism were told either "I guess you're the kind of person who likes to help others whenever you can; yes, you are a very nice and helpful person" (an inner label) or "It was good that you gave your tokens to those poor children; yes, that was a nice and helpful thing to do" (a social reward).[6] Both groups increased their sharing the next time they were given an opportunity. Later, however, the group that received the inner labels performed many more acts of altruism than the group that had received the social reward. In addition, the group that had been socially rewarded engaged in helping behavior no different from another group that had been told only, "Gee, you shared quite a bit." In other words, inner labeling appears to have a more lasting effect on children's moral behavior. The increased altruistic behavior following praise appears to wear off over time.

Considering the role of internalization in the ability to be altruistic, we should not be so surprised at these results. Telling a child that *he* is helpful teaches him about his inner empathic ability. Telling him that something he *did* was helpful only describes an act, not the child; therefore the effect wears off.

When I read this research I eagerly awaited an opportunity to try out inner labeling with my own children. My first chance arose when Ben, then about seven, mentioned at the dinner table that he was the last one on the bus for home because he had been helping another child carry her boots. *Ahah!* I thought, then cleared my throat, and said, "That's nice, Ben. You must be one of those people who like to help others." His only immediate reaction was to squirm in his chair and try to suppress a smile. At first I was afraid that all I had accomplished was to embarrass the poor kid in front of his siblings. However, later that week he performed an act of altruism so extreme and incredibly out of character that it defies any explanation other than the inner label. When getting ready to come home from school, he saw a first-grade acquaintance sitting in the wrong bus, with the right bus already having left. Ben got on that bus with him, rode with him to a point close to our home, then walked him the last six blocks to the first-grader's home. Of course, in the meantime I was becoming frazzled wondering what had happened to him. But it was easy to forgive his tardiness once I had verified what he had done. Ben performed other helpful acts in subsequent days that were less outstanding, but were still uncharacteristic of his previous behavior.

Both in the case of Ben and many of the studies, inner labeling takes place only *once*, and an increase in helpful behavior is seen. What is even more exciting is that in most experiments the inner label is given by a complete stranger. Therefore, grandparents, teachers, and even baby-sitters can have a tremendous effect on children's moral behavior. Imagine how much more effective inner labeling from parents can be. We are not only the ones our children look up to, but we can also apply inner labels on a regular basis.

Another advantage of inner labeling over praise is that inner labels are more likely to carry over to acts other than the one just performed. For example, if I had told Ben at the dinner table that helping the little girl carry her boots was a nice thing to do, he might then have been on the alert for other children who needed help carrying their belongings. Telling him that he was a helpful person freed him to act in a helpful manner in a variety of situations, not just the one that received the label. An inner label covers a much wider range of possible behaviors than a social reward.

But a number of errors can be made while attempting to use inner labels. One common error is to order a child to share, and then tell him that he shared because he was a sharing type of person. This registers within the child as baloney, because it is. The child shared because he was ordered to do so and he knows it. Applying an inner label after forced behavior will not result in increased altruistic behavior. This plausible outcome has been supported in experimental research.[7] Another cost of this error is that it decreases a parent's credibility. If parents tell a child something about his inner self he knows is not true, he is less likely to believe his parents when they use labels more appropriately.

Another error that can destroy a parent's credibility is to tell a child he is a sharing person before he has shown any indication that he plans on sharing. He might not have had any intention of sharing at that moment. Again, he may look askance at any other labels offered by his parents.

A third common error is to apply inner labels in areas of training other than prosocial behavior. Research on inner labels has concentrated on the field of altruism. Whether it can be generalized successfully to any type of personality development is not entirely certain. Even if this technique is generalizable, why wear it out on areas less crucial than moral development?

One novel situation that came to my attention involved a child (whom I will call Tim) who would not eat liver. Tim's mother (whom I will call Martha) coaxed him into taking a bite of liver, then told him, "You must be one of those kids who really likes liver." More than one logical inaccuracy occurred in this example. First of all, the initial bite was not spontaneous; it was the result of Martha's coaxing. Second, food preferences have nothing to do with altruism, so we cannot know what the eventual effect of this type of intervention will be. Third, children are human beings with their own individual taste buds, which respond to certain foods in certain ways. Telling a child he likes one food or does not like another is not going to have much long-term effect unless the preference is actually there. Tim may indeed eat a disliked food or pass by a desired food because he has discovered through Martha's behavior that this pleases her. Unfortunately, Tim's perception of Martha's credibility will eventually be impaired after repeated misapplications of this sort. Martha could just as effectively make her preferences for Tim's eating habits known by simply telling him, and would not lose his respect in so doing.

So far we have looked at the positive effect of attributing certain characteristics to children. Negative labels are also often applied to children. Some of these labels may sound familiar:

"You're always getting into trouble."
"You're a bad boy."

"You never get this right."
"When are you going to act your age?"
"You're never going to amount to anything."
"You spoiled brat."

When parents tell children that they are of questionable moral quality, children have no reason to doubt them. Putting down children may result in having a child who behaves just as he is described to himself: one of questionable moral quality.

From the inner labeling studies discussed earlier, recall the example of Johnny's spontaneously sharing his candy with Suzie. Remember that Johnny is not entirely sure why he shared and will be likely to accept whatever explanations are available. What effect would be expected at this point if the parent were to say something like, "Boy, that's a miracle!"? It would tell the child that he is inherently nonsharing, and that his sharing without prompting could not be because of any goodness to be found within himself. Parents may casually make such flip comments without ever thinking through what they mean. To children these comments have a grave meaning indeed.

Because of the way children attach labels to themselves, a good rule of thumb when criticizing or praising is to *criticize the act, and praise the child.* So if a child does a good deed, tell him he is a good boy, rather than that it was a good thing to do. When a child behaves badly, say that that was a bad thing to do, not that he is a bad boy. Since labels stick to children so well, inner labeling should be restricted to when a child has been good. Descriptions of acts stick only to the act, which a child has some control over. If he is a "bad boy," that is who he will perceive himself to be, and he will always be himself. Thus we would be creating a self-fulfilling prophecy: He would behave badly because he would believe he could do no better. Therefore, criticism should be applied to behaviors, not children.

This poses a problem when we choose to use corporal punishment. It is pretty hard, if not impossible, to convince a child who is being spanked that he is not bad. After all, *he* is the one being spanked! And since actions speak louder than words, our attempts to tell him that he is a good person would be nullified by the message of our actions: that the child deserves to be spanked, and therefore must be "bad." With this in mind, it appears that the decision to inflict pain when children misbehave must be carefully thought out. The use of corporal punishment will be discussed in greater detail in the next chapter.

ACCEPTING OFFERS OF ALTRUISM

As young children grow up into the routine of their homes, they begin to recognize when certain things need to be done. Occasionally a child will offer to do a job, often because he would like to feel he is a part of things. In reality, preparing and supervising a young child for doing most jobs is usually more trouble for the parent than performing the task herself. However, accepting these offers is an excellent technique for encouraging altruism. One study showed that children whose mothers accepted their offers for help were much more likely to offer the help again.[8]

There are several reasons accepting offers increases helping behavior. One is the phenomenon of positive reinforcement, since any behavior that results in a positive response from a parent is likely to be repeated. Another factor is that the child learns that he is capable of helping others, and gains practice at helping when his offers are accepted. In addition, the child can feel good about himself because of his discovery that he is able to recognize a need, decide how he can fulfill it, and follow through on it.

On the other hand, children's offers to help are often met with responses such as "not now," "it's already done," or "it's too hard for you." When children's offers are refused, they do not get practice showing concern for others, and may decide that they are actually incapable of acting altruistically. They may eventually decide that their help is neither wanted nor needed and offers to help will cease.

Accepting offers of altruism takes work and patience. Parents must not only supervise and assist the child trying to help, but also drop whatever they are doing at the time of the offer. It is no wonder that it is so easy for a busy parent to refuse offers without even thinking about it. A strong conscious effort may be necessary to overcome such a tendency.

Many times a child will offer to do something beyond his own capacities. Most mothers would cringe at the thought of accepting a three-year-old's offer to set the table with her antique crystal. When this type of offer occurs, the mother could suggest an alternative task for the child to perform, such as letting him put out the napkins or silverware. Cementing the discipline with an inner label ("Thank you, you are such a good helper") would help gloss over any feelings of rejection the child might have because of the changed task.

On other occasions, children will offer to do something which, if performed incorrectly, could cause some disorder but would not create a disaster. For example, a mother might have to mop up a sloppy mess if she accepted her four-year-old's offer to water the plants. In situations such as this, the mother could monitor the task by giving the child a small quantity of water at a time, and instructing him which plant to water next. Again, this does take work on the part of parents. But cultivating our children's moral development is an important and rewarding use of our time.

CONCLUSION

Inner labeling and accepting offers of altruism have a positive effect on moral development, social rewards have a limited effect, and material rewards have temporary or even negative effect. Inner labeling is by far the approach most strongly shown to get results. Parents who are accustomed to offering praise after acts of altruism may find that simply concentrating on replacing the praise with inner labels will produce fruitful results with minimal effort. Intrinsic to this technique is the necessity for parents to observe what their children are doing on a daily basis. The beauty of this factor is that it results not only in parents discovering their opportunities for applying inner labels, but also in all the good things that can happen when parents take time to be with their children.

EXERCISES

1. For each of the following praises, write an appropriate inner label. Remember, inner labels describe the child, not the behavior. Refer to page 47 if you need help. See pages 135-36 for sample responses.
   a. "Thank you for taking out the garbage. That was a helpful thing to do."
   b. "It was generous of you to give some of your allowance to the church."
   c. "How nice that you got in line quickly when it was time to get ready for gym class. That was very cooperative."
   d. "That was good that you helped Tommy when Jerry was trying to take his ball."
   e. "You children are taking turns very nicely."
2. a. Brainstorm by thinking back to various situations in which your child has spontaneously behaved altruistically, and list them on a sheet of paper. This may take some hard thinking, since it is the misbehaviors that catch our attention and stand out in our memories, rather than the appropriate behaviors.
   b. For each altruistic act, write out an appropriate inner label.
   c. Practice using the inner labels through role-playing with a spouse or friend.
3. a. Brainstorm by listing different acts of altruism your child has offered in the past. Again, this may take some hard thinking, since our usual reaction is to refuse the offer and forget about it. Using two columns, group them on a sheet of paper as shown below.

   Acceptable   Alterations
                       Necessary

   b. For those that need alteration, write out how you could change them to make them performable by your child.

CHAPTER FIVE

What to Do After Your Child Morally Offends

When my boys were five and four I frequently took them along with me to casual church gatherings. My older son, Frank, was usually content to go off and play by himself, or play on the periphery of other children's activities. Ben, on the other hand, liked to be in the middle of things. His enthusiastic nature had a way of commanding the attention of his peers. In addition, he was known to demand that things be organized according to his own "superior" judgment.

On one occasion, I was rolling bandages for the missionary barrel with several other women as we watched our children mingle. As usual, "General Ben" was directing the flow of play. However, one child had other ideas about how the toys should be distributed and took the liberty of rearranging Ben's handiwork. Ben was furious. He grabbed a toy away from the child and yelled a few choice words at him. When the child protested, Ben gave him an angry shove and sent him toppling. The child ran crying to his mother.

As the mother comforted her child, the usual chatter among the other women dwindled to a suppressed silence. The unofficial center of attention shifted away from the mother and child and drifted into my general direction. The initial shock of having my child do something so horrendously unsocialized was beginning to wear off. Ben was still standing in the play area, panting like a raging bull, the disputed toy clenched in his fist. The sweltering heat of embarrassment crept up my neck as I sensed the expectation of discipline engulfing me. The various interventions racing through my mind were at first endorsed and then rejected as I became increasingly distracted by the occasional nervous coughs and throat-clearing, which were breaking the ever deepening silence.

Finally I could no longer stand the public display of my embarrassment and indecision. I leaped out of my chair, seized Ben by the arm, and dragged him out of the room. Once I got outside earshot of the other mothers, my head began to clear. Amid the usual flurry of Ben's excuse-giving, I was able to pick an appropriate form of discipline for his transgression.

I endured many similar incidents during my boys' early years. Children can be embarrassingly selfish. Simple requests or opportunities for acts of kindness can result in responses such as "do I *have* to?" "I don't feel like it," or even "no way!" This is one of the points at which we feel the most disappointment, frustration, or even humiliation concerning our children's moral development. These highly charged emotions can interfere with our rational choosing of interventions. While we are all worked up we have to fight against reacting the way our feelings lead us. This makes self-centered, morally inappropriate behavior one of the most difficult situations to handle effectively. Chapter 2 is particularly relevant to dealing with circumstances involving moral failure.

A number of different approaches to dealing with absence of an appropriate act of altruism have been investigated in psychological research.[1] In this chapter we will look at four: punishment, reasoning, moral exhortation, and forced appropriate behavior.

PUNISHMENT

When our child perpetrates an obvious transgression, our usual reaction is to deliver some sort of consequences, generally punishment. Administering punishment serves more than the purpose of attempting to change the child's behavior. Spanking, yelling, and delivering other such consequences allows us to vent some of the emotions we feel over the child's misbehavior. Letting emotions dictate the consequences of a child's behavior is not usually the best way to choose discipline. However, it is not difficult to see how easily we could choose punishment over other ways of handling these tense situations. As we discussed in chapter 3, this seemingly automatic reflex can be channeled usefully into punishment when controlling children's short-term behavior. But as you recall, material punishment does not appear to be particularly effective in encouraging moral development, because of its focus on an external rather than internal source of guidance.

Here is an example of what can happen when a punishment system is used, involving a situation most parents have to deal with at some point. John and Marsha were having difficulty getting their son, Bob, out of bed soon enough for him to be able to get ready for school and catch his bus on time. They had been reading a lot about behavioral control of children and decided to impose a punishment scheme. For each extra "wake-up call" they had to use, Bob's bedtime for that night would be moved up half an hour. They even kept a chart of his behavior on the bathroom wall, as the thorough behaviorists they were aspiring to be would have done.

The system worked. As long as John and Marsha kept track of how many wake-up calls had been necessary, and enforced and charted the corresponding consequences, his early-morning sluggishness was cured. Unfortunately, John and Marsha eventually became sloppy in applying the system. Predictably, Bob's old habit returned. The parents' answer to this state of affairs was that they needed to train themselves better in sticking to the system.

In my view, the answer to this predicament is not so clear-cut. If all John and Marsha were trying to accomplish was to avoid morning hurry-up scenes when Bob lagged behind, simply enforcing the punishment system could have been the answer. However, if they were hoping to influence his eventual attitude toward responsibility, they would fail miserably using punishment. Once he moved away from home his motive for being responsible would be gone, and he would be left to his old habits. When parents use such coercive methods, the child is not taking responsibility for his behavior—the parents are.

Coercing desired actions has the advantage of teaching children the physical mechanics of responsibility. But unless children are also encouraged to make a personal *choice* to use those mechanics, the mechanics have little long-term value. The only effect punishment has on making choices is teaching children to choose to avoid punishment. Contrived adversity alone does not show children how to decide which behaviors are inherently right and wrong.

Kevin Leman describes another option, which may be more appropriate in this situation than contrived punishment.[2] He calls it "reality discipline." Leman suggests that punishments received by children should go along with what happens in the real world when they don't go along with what is expected of them. In the case of John and Marsha, a reality discipline would be allowing Bob to suffer the normal consequences of missing his bus. These consequences would include arranging his own transportation (John and Marsha could do it for a fee, just as adults pay bus fare when they miss their rides to work), the embarrassment of walking into class late, and the possibility of an effect on his grades (just as adults could expect an effect on their paychecks). In this manner, Bob would be receiving consequences for his actions, but they would provide incentives more congruent with the ones he needs as an adult. Although this still operates as an external focus for deciding behavior, at least the consequences received are ones that will continue when Bob leaves home.

The study on social and material rewards in chapter 4 also looked at the differences in effectiveness of material and social punishment. Children who did not share were either told "It's too bad you didn't help" (a social punishment) or had pennies taken away from them (a material punishment). Later, the children's rationale for sharing in the socially punished group included a desire to help others. Those in the materially punished group explained sharing as a way to avoid losing pennies. Again, material consequences did not seem to affect the children's internal state. They based their thinking on the external consequences they would receive: losing pennies. In addition, the social consequences again appear to have pointed out the concept of "nice" behavior, and affected the children's rationale for the behavior accordingly.

Another difficulty with punishment systems is their connection with punitiveness, which is the act of purposely causing some form of discomfort for a person. Punishment is intended to change behavior for the better, which is certainly a sound motive. Unfortunately, anything that causes pain, discomfort, or unpleasantness for a person is also punitive.

Thomas Lickona, in his book *Raising Good Children,* discusses which moral lessons children pick up from various punitive methods.[3] He gives several possible parental responses to a situation where little boys are throwing rocks in front of moving cars on the road, and points out what children learn from them:

Parent's Response	*Child's Moral Learning*
Shaming: "Don't you know any better than that? Throwing stones at cars is something we'd expect from a 3-year-old!"	"Mom and Dad don't think very much of me. I guess I am pretty dumb."
Embarrassment: "What kind of home will people think you come from?"	"I should be worried about what the neighbors think—not about what could happen to a driver."
Intimidation: "Do you realize what could happen if a policeman saw you doing that?"	"If I'm gonna throw stones at cars, I'd better be sure nobody's looking."
Punishment: "You lose all TV for a week. I hope this will be a lesson for you."	"I'd better not throw stones again if I know what's good for me."

Notice that none of these moral learning responses teaches the child to care what happens to others. The child's internal workings are activated defensively: "How do I protect myself against possible consequences concerning *my* self-esteem, *my* appearance to the neighbors, *my* entanglements with the law, and *my* television habits?"

W. Hugh Missildine, a prominent psychiatrist, best describes the potential emotional effects of punitiveness:

> Many people sincerely believe that punitiveness is actually necessary to teach the child "discipline." They want the child to obey them without hesitation and do what they consider desirable—and to respect them. But punitiveness by itself is nearly a total failure as a teaching method for discipline and nearly 100 percent successful in teaching disrespect, hate and fear.
>
> It teaches a respect for power and creates a desire for power in order to retaliate. But parents want loving respect—and when they get hateful respect, they are both hurt and more punitive. We pay a fantastic price for the end results of parental punitiveness in outlays for social services that range from child care agencies to psychiatric hospitals and elaborate police and prison systems. Financially, this amounts to millions yearly. But this doesn't begin to match the misery that punitiveness wreaks in human lives.[4]

Clearly, these consequences of punitive methods are not what we are trying to accomplish with our children. Yet punishment is one of the most pervasive themes found in childrearing manuals. This pervasiveness may be owing to an aspect of punishment that manuals generally do not discuss: It offers tremendous reward for the parent. Punishment or the threat of punishment is very effective in getting our children to do what *we* want them to do, and right now! By using punishment, we get our way. Little wonder, then, that we rely so heavily on it, in spite of the objections that may try to surface from our own inner empathic selves. Obviously, this does not justify ignoring all of the negative side effects experienced by the punished child. Considering the fact that there are alternatives to punitiveness, we stand cautioned to take a closer look at them and curtail our focus on punishment.

CORPORAL PUNISHMENT

One of the most hotly debated issues in childrearing history has been whether or not to spank, strike, or otherwise inflict pain on a child who has misbehaved. This issue's sizzling nature fuels my immediate impulse to wriggle my way around it and pretend it doesn't exist. But I can't effectively present my case for childrearing without explaining my perspectives and biases on a form of discipline so prevalently relied on.

My advice on this topic is *not* a direct product of specific absolute realities, spectacularly supported research findings, or revelations from God. What I am about to present is my opinion. This opinion is based on an amalgam formed from my exposure to child development research, parents, children, the clinical insights of other mental health professionals, and my own parenting experience and religious beliefs.

Perhaps the best way to go about presenting my position is to explain how I got here. I began by constructing a list of the advantages and disadvantages of corporal punishment.

The biggest advantage of corporal punishment is that children are highly motivated to avoid it. We all try to avoid pain. Careful kitchen behavior is a product of learning to avoid pain: We only have to burn ourselves once before we incorporate all sorts of cautions into our kitchen practices.

A second advantage to inflicting pain is that some classical conditioning can occur. If you recall from the discussion in chapter 1, classical conditioning results in a feeling being experienced in the presence of a previously neutral stimulus, because in the past, the neutral stimulus has been paired with something that would have naturally produced such a feeling. In the case of corporal punishment, if spankings are repeatedly employed just as a child is reaching for a forbidden object or engaging in some specific unwanted behavior, the feelings of apprehension a child would experience when anticipating a spanking will also be experienced just as he thinks about or begins to engage in the undesired behavior. He will therefore avoid the undesired behavior because of the discomfort of the apprehension.

A third advantage is that it is easy to administer. After you decide that a spanking is in order, you don't have to stop and think, *Now, what would be the best way to explain this moral lesson?* until perhaps after the spanking, when you have had some time to think and an outlet for cooling down.

A fourth advantage is that scripture appears to support corporal punishment. References to the use of the "rod" for discipline are scattered throughout Scripture.

My list of disadvantages to corporal punishment began with taking a second look at each of the advantages. The first disadvantage is that the motivation to avoid pain is so strong, the child may engage in other undesirable behaviors in order to avoid it—such as lying about something he did or cheating or stealing to cover up the evidence of an offense that would call for a spanking.

The second disadvantage, which concerns classical conditioning, reminds me of a story about a British friend of mine who described how she disciplined her cocker spaniel as a puppy. She explained that she used a rolled-up newspaper to swat him with, rather than her hand, because she did not want the dog to connect the feeling of pain with human contact. "And he hasn't given us a moment's trouble since he was a pup," bragged my friend. "However," she added, "he never has particularly cared for the man who sells the fliers."

The problem is that you are never quite sure which stimulus is going to become connected with the feelings of apprehension. The stimulus most likely to become attached is whatever was present or happening in the environment immediately before or during the spanking. The traditional spanking procedure has been to remove the child from the situation, explain to him what he did wrong, and then deliver the spanking. Sometimes spankings are not given until hours after the transgression just because the parents don't find out about the offense until long after it has taken place. In both these circumstances, the spanking has been administered so long after the undesired behavior and so far away from the setting in which it took place that there is no possibility of the feeling of apprehension being connected with what the parents want to be changed. Instead, the child learns to become apprehensive when around his parents, since they were the ones he was most aware of as he received the spanking.

The third disadvantage, concerning the ease of application, is that it is too easy. It can become the primary mode of discipline and become inappropriately used just because so little thought is required to produce the action of spanking. It also seems to flow naturally from being angry, which can result in our hitting our child just because his actions have angered us.

The fourth disadvantage, concerning biblical teachings, is that there is no reason to believe that the "rod" passages were meant to be taken literally. I have always found it difficult to connect the concept of love to striking children with objects. I realize that a number of parenting manuals have gone to great lengths to rationalize such a connection, and that these arguments generally suggest that the ends justify the means. But what matters is how the *child* feels when he is struck, rather than what the parent is trying to convince herself she is doing as she spanks her child. Spanked children do not feel love. If they do, the classic model of masochism may be well on its way to becoming set in place.

A fifth disadvantage is the legacy of research, which has shown that parents who become child batterers almost always were spanked as children. Could it be that how we treat our children will contribute to some dire consequence for our grandchildren?

A sixth disadvantage was discussed in chapter 4. If a child is spanked, he will believe he is bad, and inner labeling to the contrary will not be believed.

The remaining disadvantages to corporal punishment are the same ones that apply to punishment in general: It encourages a self-centered, external focus, behavior change tends only to last as long as the threat of punishment is present, it doesn't tell the child what the appropriate behavior would be, it does not let the child take responsibility for his actions, it teaches children to respect power rather than respect the parent, and it places an emotional rift between parent and child.

The conclusion I came to as I reviewed all of these data was that corporal punishment is probably something to be avoided. But I also recognized that with some children in some situations, physical pain seems to be the only thing that catches their attention.

My advice is this:

1. Corporal punishment should be used extremely sparingly. If possible, don't use it at all.
2. Corporal punishment should be restricted to the very young. Older children have the verbal skills to be able to be reasoned with. If you feel you must punish, older children can be punished in a variety of more creative and even reality-based ways that will not have as many unfortunate side effects as being spanked.
3. When you spank, restrict yourself to a single swat on your child's bottom, which is administered *while* the child is engaging in the undesired behavior. Remember that if you leave a mark, it is considered to be abuse. Spanking at a time interval that is anything more than a few seconds after the offense or is in a different setting from where the offense took place should be eliminated, because there aren't enough benefits to outweigh the side effects.
4. Decide ahead of time what a spankable offense is. This way you guard against letting your anger cloud your reasoning while you are deciding whether or not to spank.
5. Offenses that call for a spanking include those behaviors that it is extremely important be changed and that have not responded to less severe forms of discipline. I suggest that this list of offenses be restricted to activities that can be dangerous to the child or to others, and to behaviors in a young child that take him so far out of necessary parental control that no other method appears to reach him.

Again, this advice is an opinion, which is based on my evaluation of a number of facts. As one of my supervisors used to tell me, "The facts won't tell you what you *should* do, but they'll tell you what will *happen* if you do it." To spank or not to spank is a value judgment, and I encourage the reader to use such relevant facts while making his or her own judgment on whether or not to use corporal punishment.

REASONING

Children do not reason the same way that adults do. The world is still very new to them, and overwhelming in its complexity. Children find safety in living by simple rules, preferably one rule at a time. Learning to think outside one line of reasoning is an immense task for them.

One of my colleagues shared with me this story about how to handle difficult teacher-child relationships. A speaker my friend had heard had suggested that the power struggles could be broken up if the teacher did something bizarre and out of character. As an example, he described a situation where the entire class was doing assignments except for one problem student who was whooping it up. The teacher knelt down beside the student, looked him in the eye, and asked "Want to buy a dead duck?" The student was bewildered for a few moments, but eventually started in on his work.

I thought this tale was hilarious and I was just sure that Ben, then eight, would enjoy it, too. I told him the whole story barely containing my laughter, and gave in to a tear-spangled guffaw when I got to the part about the dead duck. As I dabbed at the moisture from my eyes I noticed that Ben was still just standing there, watching me intently.

"Well?" I said. "Don't you think that was funny?"

"So how much was the duck?"

Ben just could not follow the humor in the story because he was tracking a single theme—the sale of a dead duck—as would be expected from a child his age. In order to understand the joke, he would have had to take into account the second theme—the teacher's motive of trying to confuse the student long enough for him to forget his antics and do his work. Recently, I repeated this story to Ben in order to obtain his permission to write about it. As an eleven-year-old he not only understood the humor in the technique, but also laughed when he heard what his own response to hearing the story had been. As an older child he was able to take into account more than one theme, and the humor hit home.

When children misbehave, they are trapped into their usual one line of thinking. They are generally thinking about their own desires or involvement in the situation. The effect their actions have on others involves considering both their perspective and the feelings of others. This type of reasoning does not come naturally for children, since there is more than one set of rules to consider.

We can encourage children to consider the feelings of others by explaining to them how their selfish reactions affect the others who are involved. Such explanations are likely to cause them some discomfort and encourage them to develop their empathic selves. This is especially true in young children if the parent's facial expression illustrates extreme feeling. Research has shown that presenting emotion is especially effective with very young children (ages one-and-a-half to two-and-a-half).[5] They are much more likely to act considerately after being presented with explanations if the parent's tone of voice shows the hurt, anger, or other emotion the victim of the nonaltruistic act was experiencing.

For example, if Johnny refuses to share his candy with Suzie, a parent might put on a sad face and emotionally say, "That's too bad. I'll bet that candy looks really yummy to Suzie. She must be really unhappy that you are not sharing it with her." On the very young, who have not yet been trained to ignore their empathic ability, the impact is sometimes so strong that the child immediately shares, or even begins to cry.

Another version would be, "I'll bet you would be sad if Suzie had the candy and didn't share with you." Making him think about what his own feelings are like hits him where his heart is. Such comments help the child see that others are like himself. This gives him a greater appreciation for what other people feel.

The design of this intervention is threefold:

1. The child is made aware that others have feelings.
2. The child is made aware that his actions have caused others to be in distress.
3. The child feels self-induced guilt over the consequences of his inconsiderate behavior.

These three factors expand the child's line of thinking. A new set of rules is made evident, and is reinforced by the child's own natural empathy. Research has indeed supported the relationship between this type of reasoning and children's eventual concern for others.[6] Once children are fully aware of how their behavior affects others, their empathy will deliver self-inflicted guilt if they cause distress in others. They therefore conform to caring behavior in order to avoid the pain of guilt feelings.

MORAL EXHORTATION

Moral exhortation goes one step further than reasoning. Reasoning helps the child understand how his actions affect others; moral exhortation tells the child precisely what he should or should not do about it. Research has shown that children whose mothers explain to them why they should not have been inconsiderate are more likely to be altruistic in the future.[7] Again, it is important that an emotional element be attached to the exhortation. For example, telling a child "It is not nice to kick; you should never kick people" will not be as effective as adding an emotional "You hurt Mary when you kicked her." This is the same as the rationale behind techniques discussed earlier: Putting a child in touch with his empathic, emotional feelings compels him to consider the feelings of others when deciding how to act.

It is important to note that a simple "Don't do that," without explaining why, does not usually work very well. The study concerning the one-and-a-half-year-olds to two-and-a-half-year-olds showed that being told not to do something was actually negatively correlated with future acts of altruism. In other words, the more that two-year-olds are told simply "no," the *less* altruistically they will behave. This is no surprise to mothers of two-year-olds. Oppositional behavior is a way of life for this age group! However, adding an emotionally charged explanation to saying no communicates with the two-year-old on an emotional, empathic level and appears to override the standard, thought-based reaction of challenging whatever Mommy says.

With older children, the effect is not as immediate as with younger children. If an older child is told that he should behave in a certain way, chances are he will at first balk, if for no other reason than just to see what sort of reaction he will get. Over time, this tendency diminishes, and increased altruistic behavior eventually takes place.[8]

The familiar quip "Do as I say, not as I do" is relevant to this technique. The humor behind the saying is that people have a tendency to repeat what they see others actually doing, even if what these others are exhorting is the opposite. Research with children in this dilemma shows that children react similarly.[9] In conditions where an adult acts one way and then tells a child to act in another way, the child inevitably uses the adult's actions as a blueprint for future behavior. Apparently hypocrisy is such an obvious phenomenon that even a child can recognize it, if perhaps only subconsciously.

Looking to what others do in deciding which behavioral pattern to follow is actually modeling, which we will discuss in depth in the following chapter. Modeling alone tends to be more effective than exhortation alone. Although having an altruistic model does encourage moral growth on its own, a combined method where noncontradictory modeling and exhortation support one another is superior. This is because a model only provides an example of something being done. Adding a moral exhortation to the modeled behavior illustrates for the child the principle of caring about others, which can be built into the child's inner beliefs. Sharing motives orally is discussed in greater detail in chapter 6.

Another important element of moral exhortations is their generalizability. As mentioned in the last chapter, one of the reasons that inner labels are more effective than praise in producing change is that praise is associated only with the *act* receiving praise. Inner labels (for example, being generous) can be applied by the child to a number of behaviors requiring generosity. This same principle is involved with moral exhortations.[10] The exhortation "You should share your Tinkertoys with Bobby; that is the right thing to do. He will be sad if you don't" will increase the likelihood that the nonsharing child will share Tinkertoys with Bobby in the future. However, adding to this exhortation the more general statement "It is usually best to share your things with others" allows the child to apply the lesson to many different sharing situations with many different people, not just to the immediate circumstance.

Ideally, then, moral exhortations should contain the following elements:

1. They should tell the child what he should or should not do.
2. They should include an emotionally presented reference to the feelings of or consequences for the other person or persons involved.
3. They should be supported by the adult's behavior.
4. They should include a generalized statement that reaches outside the immediate situation.

Here is another illustration. Ten-year-old Robby is mesmerized by his older brother Fred's new ten-speed bicycle. He decides that he will "borrow" it to go impress one of his little friends. In the meantime Fred comes home. Upon discovering that the bike is missing, he becomes understandably upset. The parents are about ready to call the police when Robby coasts nonchalantly up the driveway. There are several moral exhortations the parents could use:

"You should never take things without asking. Just think of how upset you would be if that were your bike and you came home and found it missing."

"You should always consider the feelings of others before you take their things. Fred was so upset today he couldn't even do his homework. Now he will have to do his homework tonight."

"We would certainly never take your things without asking. You would be upset if we did."

"Poor Fred was afraid he would never see his bike again. Just look at how upset he is because of what you did. You should always think about the feelings of others."

Here is an example of reasoning and moral exhortation gone awry. Janet had come to pick up her three-year-old son, Teddy, at his friend's house. Teddy did not want to go home and protested loudly, refusing to budge. Finally Janet picked him up in order to carry him out the door. In retaliation, Teddy began pounding his fists on her shoulders and face. Janet proceeded to explain to him why he shouldn't do that as she struggled to carry him out the door. Teddy continued to pummel her with blows all the while she was talking. In self-defense she set him down and tried to get away from him, but Teddy ran behind her all the way home, taking another swing at her whenever he got close enough. Janet reported that she had completely lost control of Teddy after that incident.

Reasoning and moral exhortation did not work out in this situation, and there are some clear reasons why. First, very young children still have the "no" reflex well intact. We could have predicted that the hitting would indeed increase if all the mother was doing was delivering sophisticated versions of the concept of no. If she had confronted him emotionally, as we discussed earlier, she would have had at least some chance of communicating. However, there still wouldn't be any guarantee that the hitting would stop, since moral interventions by definition do not always get instant results.

Second, it is highly questionable whether reasoning would be the appropriate intervention for this particular situation. Reasoning and moral exhortation are long-range interventions and are not necessarily going to get instant results. Repeatedly hitting other human beings, no matter who they are, is something that needs to be stopped immediately. A child's entire moral framework will eventually center on his caring and empathy for others. Such an extreme display of aggression and lack of respect for another's feelings cannot go unaltered, and coercive measures are definitely called for. Using a moral intervention for such a behavior borders on entertaining the absurd.

How did Janet go astray? We can't know all the history that led to this one vignette. However, I would speculate that she had a bad case of "black-and-white"-ism, where she saw any given technique as being all good or all powerful, and any contenders as therefore all bad or useless. Life is never that simple. As with any other life issue, the truth lies somewhere between. Different techniques have their greatest power in different situations; none necessarily exceeds the others overall. Janet's downfall appears to lie within an assumption that since reasoning is a good technique, it is the only technique that should be used; and any other alternatives, such as coercion methods, would be useless. Saying that coercion has no place because reasoning can sometimes do the trick is just as ludicrous as saying that reasoning has no value because of its more limited coercive power. Each has its place.

DISGUISED MORAL EXHORTATION

A number of children seem to be especially inclined toward doing the opposite of what they think we want them to do. This particular breed of child can prove to be exasperatingly resilient in rejecting our stated values. When faced with this sort of childrearing predicament, we have to find some other way of getting our message across without the obviousness of our imperatives showing through. Here is where we get sneaky. We disguise our exhortations, so that it looks as if the child has come up with our values all on his own.

Lickona's *Raising Good Children* calls this "ask-don't-tell" reasoning. Instead of telling the child what he should do and why, we ask him questions that will lead to the principle.

For example, when our child throws a tantrum in the store because we won't buy a toy he wants, our moral exhortation might be "Tantrums make people angry. We should always think about how our actions affect others, and try not to hurt them on purpose." The ask-don't-tell approach would involve asking the child what *he* thinks:

"How do you think I feel when you act like this?"
"Would you like it if someone you know acted like this when you wouldn't buy him whatever he wanted?"
"What would you say if you were the parent right now?"
"What would be a good rule to remember when you feel like throwing a tantrum?"

Naturally, this sort of technique is going to work much better with an older child than a younger one. The younger child has less control over his emotions and is not as likely to set them aside in order to delve into reasoning processes. He also needs a little time to accumulate a library of rationales.

Ask-don't-tell enables the older child to think things through for himself. The more practice he gets at reasoning, the more likely it is that he will be able to initiate reasoning on his own at times of decision making.

In addition, asking a child to think something out on his own shows him that you think highly of his intelligence. Imagine that you made a small error in some area of your work. How would you feel if your employer gave you a five-minute lecture on why you goofed, when it was actually an explanation so simple that any novice could see the error once it was pointed out? You would feel put down, insulted, and perhaps even trodden upon. You might even get defensive, denying that the error really mattered. On the other hand, if your employer good-naturedly commented, "See something wrong here, Ms. Jones?" you would analyze the material, notice the mistake, and correct it. You would probably feel grateful that the error was pointed out before it caused any real problems, and would feel good about your own analytical and corrective skills.

Letting children find the answers serves the same purposes. They see that you believe in them. They discover their own reasoning processes, and they feel good about their abilities. Since they get to state the principle themselves, there is less likelihood of defensiveness. Best of all, it shows them that they can look inside themselves to find secure inner standards for guiding their behavior.

FORCED APPROPRIATE BEHAVIOR

Sometimes when children fail to be considerate, parents force their child to follow through on the appropriate behavior. For example, if Johnny refused to share his candy with Suzie, his parents might order him to share. Forcing the issue not only gives the parents the satisfaction of seeing the correct behavior displayed, but also appears to result in an increase in similar behavior.[11] The apparent success of this method may be owing to the same reasons as is the success of accepting acts of altruism. The child gains practice in sharing, and may gain internal rewards for having done so.

However, one group of researchers pointed out that in most of the experiments where commands were successfully used, no negative consequences were threatened if the child did not comply.[12] The commands were stated more as rules to be followed, as in a game, rather than an authority-based absolute that would be enforced with coercive means. In other words, the children were not acting out of a fear of punishment; therefore, internalization was possible. When parents make commands, no mention of a threat is necessary for the child to understand that he is in hot water if he does not follow through on what is expected of him. Therefore, when parents make commands, fear of punishment is the child's likely motivator. Since fear of punishment leads children to look outside themselves for direction, internalization will not take place. For this reason, forced appropriate behavior is probably a poor choice as an intervention for nonmoral behavior.

Forcing children has other drawbacks. Another study in which children were forced to share showed in the posttest that *stealing* took place among the children who had been forced.[13] It is hypothesized that these children felt resentment over having something taken away from them that was rightfully theirs. They found a way of getting even, or acting out that anger, by stealing. Such possible side effects suggest that forced appropriate behavior may not necessarily be wise. Possibly the stealing is only an oppositional reaction and would fade away over time, as happens when children balk at moral exhortations. However, when children receive the payoff of immediate ill-gotten gratification, the realization of this reward may stick around long after the reactance has worn off. Thus parents who force sharing could unwittingly be encouraging their child to steal! Considering the effectiveness that moral exhortations and reasoning can have in the same type of situation, perhaps we would be better off to use them as interventions.

CONCLUSION

Reasoning and moral exhortation are among the most effective interventions in dealing with lack of altruism. Forced appropriate behavior can result in immediate appropriate behavior, but may not internalize and can have harmful side effects involving rebellion. Social punishment can at least make a child aware that the values of good and bad exist. Material punishment appears to be detrimental because of its focus on external consequences.

As in the case of consequences following altruism, parents who are used to intervening after inappropriate behaviors can do well by simply plugging a new reaction into the intervention slot. Instead of punishing or forcing appropriate behavior after a nonaltruistic act, we can help our children by making greater use of responses that include reasoning and moral exhortation.

EXERCISES

Below are several situations where children have acted nonaltruistically. Write a moral exhortation that could be used as an intervention. Remember the four elements:

　　a. It tells the child what he should or should not do.
　　b. It refers to the feelings of or consequences to others.
　　c. It is not contradictory to the parent's behavior.
　　d. It includes a general statement concerning the area of altruism involved.

Page 137 offers sample responses.

1. Sarah is riding her tricycle. After a while her friend, Tanya, asks if she can have a turn. Sarah refuses.
2. Jimmy needs help carrying his toys out to the sandbox. Rather than helping out, Timmy plays with the toys Jimmy has already brought out.
3. Mother tells the children to wash up for lunch. Dick and Jane wash up and sit down, but Sally continues playing with her dolls. The others end up sitting and waiting for their lunch until Sally finally follows through.
4. Betty has lost her red crayon. She sees that Jenny still has one and she takes ownership.
5. Lucy has fallen down and skinned her knee. Rather than staying and comforting her, Tiffany runs off to play with the other children.

Below are sample parental reactions to children's misbehavior. Rewrite them into questions in the tradition of the ask-don't-tell method[14]: Sample responses can be found on pages 137-38.

1. "That kind of language around the house is totally unacceptable!"
2. "You're not cooperating the least bit!"
3. "You're causing a lot of tension by your whining and complaining!"
4. "Tell your sister you're sorry you hit her and promise you won't do it again."
5. "Stop fighting and take turns!"
6. "When you make demands instead of asking nicely, I don't feel like doing anything for you."
7. "You can help by bringing some of the groceries."

Chapter Six

Modeling and Empathy Training

Monkey see, monkey do." This familiar saying has been around much longer than the research in social learning theory of the past few decades. People have always been aware that a good deal of learning takes place just from watching others. Most of us can recall someone we admire so strongly that we have attempted to imitate that person's mannerisms. Children also learn by observing others. They can demonstrate whole new sequences of behavior, such as singing a new song or playing a new game, just by having watched someone else do them first.[1]

Many experts agree that a large portion, if not most, of socialization takes place by watching others. Moral training is no exception. Research has shown that children who first watch adults perform charitable acts are more likely to behave charitably themselves than if they did not see an adult share.[2] Children look to what adults do in deciding what is morally correct, and pattern their own behavior accordingly. Since the adults children most frequently watch are their parents, we will be looking more at parental behavior in this chapter than the behavior of the child.

ATTITUDES TOWARD AUTHORITY

One of the most important attitudes we can teach our children is respect for authority. Without it, a child will have difficulty developing respect for the authority of society or his chosen religious orientation. Some of this is taught by how we react to our children's attitude toward our own authority as parents. It is not unusual for children to try out various disrespectful behaviors such as yelling at parents, direct disobedience, or perhaps even hitting parents. This brand of extreme defiance cannot be left unchallenged, or our children may assume that authority figures are something to be ignored or abused. Children do need to have an opportunity to express their anger and frustration over not getting their own way, even though such feelings are not the deciding factor in resolving situations. We need to listen to our child's feelings so he will know that feelings are all right.

The coercive type of discipline we choose should center on *how* the child expresses his feelings. His saying that our discipline makes him angry is not disrespectful. His letting his anger guide him to refuse to do something society requires of us all is not just disrespectful; it can also result in social chaos.

However, the majority of a child's eventual attitudes toward authority are developed by watching how his parents react to authority. Examining our own interactions with authority can show us what we are teaching our children. Do we demonstrate our respect for authority in daily living? Or are our life-styles characterized by not-so-subtle forms of rebellion, which our children can easily observe?

For example, modeling obedience is difficult while we are driving 62 miles an hour in a 55-mile-an-hour zone. If our child noticed this and asked about it, we might comment "Well, they don't give out tickets unless you're going at least 65." Although this explanation might alleviate the child's fears of being pulled over by the police, it would be detrimental to his moral development. It models for him an external basis of control for behavior—the police force—rather than an internal set of values that respects authority because of its establishment by the majjority's desires. The result would be a child who would only cooperate with authority because of the consequences he might receive, and who would be discouraged from developing his inner belief system.

There are many other ways we can model lack of respect for authority. Two good examples are how we react to government and to God. Do we speak angrily of government as a "them" who are out to control and restrict us, and as an entity to be rebelled against? Or do we recognize government as a system we are a working and cooperative part of, regardless of whether we agree with how it is presently being run? Do we choose our moral behaviors according to any private meanings we may have attributed to God out of situational convenience? Or do we speak of our moral choices in terms of a specific body of religious teachings, which we have chosen to adopt as our internal standard? In both of these examples, the disobedient alternative models an external, self-serving attitude toward authority. The well-adjusted alternative models an internal value system, which has been accepted because it takes into account the rights of all.

As was pointed out in chapter 5, we can voice moral exhortations indefinitely, if we so choose. But unless we are as obedient to authority as we tell our children to be, exhortations will fall on deaf ears.

ANGER AND AGGRESSION

A substantial body of research exists on how children learn to handle aggression in socially acceptable ways.[3] One of the landmark studies showed that children who watch an adult behave aggressively when angry will react in the same way when they become frustrated.[4] If we yell obscenities, slam doors, throw things, or strike objects or people when we are angry, we can be assured that our children will eventually express their anger in the same fashion. On the other hand, if we express our anger through assertive self-expression and find reasonable ways to resolve anger-provoking situations, we can expect our children to handle their own anger in a way that is more socialized.

Many people have a difficult time knowing what to do with anger. Because of its intense, explosive nature, many people believe it is the same as aggression. It certainly *feels* directed toward others. When we cannot distinguish the difference between aggression and anger, chances are good that we will either allow hostility to control our behavior, or we will see our angry feelings as being unacceptable and will suppress them. Neither alternative is healthy.

R. E. Alberti and Michael L. Emmons have written an excellent book that teaches an understanding of the difference between anger and aggression.[5] *Your Perfect Right: A Guide to Assertive Behavior* has been called the "bible of assertiveness training." It helps people distinguish the differences between anger and aggression by explaining anger as a feeling, and aggression as only one of many types of behavior we can choose from in order to dispel angry feelings.

Aggression can manifest itself in a number of ways. *General* aggression is found in the person who places few bounds on her anger. She is accustomed to bullying others to get her way. She typically does not acknowledge her anger as being self-induced. If she is angry, she sees others as being responsible for having made her become that way, and feels justified in abusing others because they "deserve" it. While childrearing, the generally aggressive parent has a tendency to see children's undesirable behaviors as intentionally inducing her anger, and is likely to be overpunitive. As we discussed earlier, overpunitiveness causes children to grow up to be just as hostile and vengeful as their parents. As models, generally aggressive parents teach their children that if you are angry, you have the right to take it out on others.

Situational aggression is practiced by the person who sees the general inappropriateness or drawbacks of unleashed aggression and tends to use it only as a last resort. Usually it is only under certain circumstances that the situationally aggressive person loses control. For example, this sort of person may take a lot of flak from people until she can no longer stand it. At this point the person blows up, acting just as obnoxious as the generally aggressive person. As parents they provide a confusing model for their children. They may docilely put up with certain behaviors for months, never telling their children that the irritating behavior is unacceptable to them. Then out of nowhere, they respond with a blow-up, which their bewildered children had no idea was coming. This inconsistency teaches children to ignore parents' rules, since nine times out of ten the rules are not enforced. As a model, the situationally aggressive parent teaches that you save up your hurts. When you have enough to use as an excuse to vent anger on others, you can explode at will.

Passive aggression is the choice of the person who won't come out and say when she is angry, but by golly, she'll find a way to get even. For example, a wife may tell her husband that she doesn't mind at all if on one certain evening he comes home from work an hour late. However, she makes sure that his dinner is cold or burnt, rather than telling her husband that she would prefer that he come straight home. When she doesn't agree with what her husband says or does, she may direct sugary sweet statements toward her children along the lines of "that silly Daddy! He really doesn't know what he's talking about, does he?" Sarcastic innuendoes are common, since if the victim asks if the passive-aggressive person is upset, the anger can be denied: "I was just being funny!" The passive-aggressive model teaches the child that he is not supposed to say directly that he is angry, but he can sure relieve his anger by finding indirect ways to even the score.

All three of these aggressive types are maladaptive. None of these interactional styles results in satisfied people. What people really want is to have the sources of anger change or go away. Unfortunately, the aggressive person's actions infuriate others, which decreases the likelihood that others will go out of their way to accommodate him. Even if others do not develop vengeful feelings toward an aggressive person, they often do not know how to please him, since his focus is on aggressing rather than directly communicating needs or feelings. Problem solving in the face of aggression is impossible.

Alberti and Emmons' main thrust is how to express feelings assertively, rather than aggressively. They define assertiveness as "behavior which enables a person to act in his or her own best interests, to stand up for herself or himself without undue anxiety, to express honest feelings comfortably, or to exercise personal rights without denying the rights of others."[6] The assertive person therefore expresses his anger without demanding a scalp from every person who crosses him. He makes sure he has enough relevant information in a situation before passing a judgment. He states "I am angry" rather than "you make me angry," thereby taking responsibility for his own role in the situation. He explains to people precisely what it is they are doing that bothers him, without demanding that they immediately conform to his desires. He works together with others in order to come to consensus solutions, even though it means he will not always get his way.

If you are uncomfortable about the way you express yourself and suspect that you may be treading on the toes of others when you do, Alberti and Emmons' book deserves your full attention. In addition to learning how to provide a good role model for your child, you will feel better about yourself. As chapter 2 reminded us, we all slip up occasionally. But we can always endeavor to do better!

The expression of anger is not the only model of emotion we provide for our children. Modeling love and affection is also important.

LOVE

Our parents were only human, and as might be expected, they had their human faults. In addition to modeling love, they modeled a good number of the usual shortcomings, including those in the areas of anger, aggression, and authority attitudes discussed earlier. Our immediate impulses often reflect attitudes that have been passed down from parent to child for many generations. It is not unusual for us to find that we are not even aware of the patterns we are passing along. W. Hugh Missildine's *Your Inner Child of the Past* is an excellent source for discovering familial patterns and tendencies.[7]

Our children need love models. As we discussed in chapter 3, the most important attribute of our existence is our ability to experience love and compassion. However, it is not enough that a child simply experience compassion. He must also know how to express it. Feeling upset that another child has lost his candy is insufficient; relieving both his anxiety and the other child's by sharing his own candy with him is an idea he may need to see by example.

How much compassion toward others do we demonstrate?

When we see others hurting do we say "that's too bad" and move on about our own business, or do we take the time to listen to their hurts and offer our support? When we see persons in need, do we just pray for a solution, or do we seek ways to help them find what they need? When a confused driver tries to cut in front of us in heavy traffic, do we make things difficult for him and give him dirty looks, or do we make way to accommodate him? When family members all want to watch different television programs at the same time, do we begin a power struggle of survival of the fittest, or do we selflessly concede to the wishes of a weaker family member? When we have a complaint against others, do we speak negatively and judgmentally of their character, or do we seek the understanding and strength necessary to love them more?

Children are keen observers, and if you keep your eyes open, you may discover a junior version of your own behavior coming back at you. I frequently use inner labeling techniques with my young daughter, Bridie. One day after I picked her up at her friend's house I informed her that I had a surprise at home for her. Delighted, she exclaimed, "You're real nice, Mom! That makes people happy when you give them surprises!"

Children watch how we treat them, and use our actions as a behavioral guide in deciding how they will treat others. Unfortunately, few parents are able to say that they treat their children the way they would like their children to treat others. Children are often told to stop bugging parents while they are trying to do something, are treated as if their ideas were not important, are yelled at over relatively unimportant transgressions, and may even be served hot dogs while the adults are having steaks. This is certainly not how most adults would treat their friends! The issue is respect. If children are treated as worthy individuals they will learn to see others as worthy of love. If they are treated as second-class citizens they will recognize neither the worth of others nor the need to treat others as being as valuable as they are.

How parents treat each other is another arena of learning. If parents are constantly belittling or angrily disagreeing with each other, the child will assume that such behavior is the correct way to treat parents, and will treat them the same way.

Furthermore, when children become adults and have families of their own, they will be likely to treat their spouses in the same abusive patterns they witnessed as children. When, as parents, we model mutual respect for each other, our children learn to show respect toward us and others as well.

The concept "charity begins at home" could not be any more true than it is in showing love in the home. We can never be perfect love models. However, we can find peace in knowing that any bits of love we can display before our children will not go to waste. Modeling love ensures that our children will at least have a blueprint for choosing loving behavior in their own lives.

WHAT TO DO WHEN WE BLOW IT

Parenting is a rough job. On top of the usual adult pressures we face, it seems as if we are also supposed to apply saintly compassion and the wisdom of Solomon while dealing with the seemingly trivial dilemmas children often place before us. At other times we feel overwhelmed by the complexity of resolving our children's uncomfortable situations and problems. It is not hard to see how we can let our own human imperfections of character, feelings, and frustrations guide our parenting, rather than think our way through to the best way to react. Because of this human frailty, we parents often goof.

Usually our children either consciously or subconsciously sense that we are being unfair. For example, we may invest a good deal of energy in telling our children not to yell and scream at each other, then turn around and yell at them ourselves. Occasionally we may punish the wrong child. We may punish a child for doing something he did not know was wrong. Sometimes when problems arise, we do not give our children sufficient "air time" for them to present their case. At other times we may not take our children's feelings into account at all, just because their wishes don't fit in with adult realities.

Although children may sense our failures, they do not often address them directly. Children see us as being all-powerful and all-knowing. Even if they are internally raging over the injustice to which they are being subjected, they externally accept their mistreatment as valid, since they believe that authority figures can do no wrong. Unless we point out to children our errors in judgment, they will accept injustice as justice. They will make the same bad choices themselves, because their authority figures have essentially put their stamp of approval on them.

We often confess errors and ask forgiveness when we are dealing with our peers. Unfortunately, we do not always apply these same principles when dealing with our children. We tend to experience some hesitance in putting ourselves in an imperfect light in front of our children. Ironically, part of this hesitance is owing to wanting to be a "good example" for them. If we present ourselves as imperfect, we may ask, how can we trust that they will accept our exhortations of right and wrong? Another part of this hesitance comes from a deeper, emotional level. There is an inner part of ourselves that demands authority over our children just because we are their parents.

Alice Miller explores these feelings and explains them in relation to our own childhood experiences.[8] In our authoritarian culture, parents are nurtured as being absolute authorities over their children. Being a child means having no control or power, and being entirely subject to the desires of parents. Imagine how we would feel as adults if we had absolutely no power over our lives. For adults, this type of treatment is typically reserved for prison-like situations. Think of the relief prisoners must feel when they finally get out on their own. What a joy it must be for them to be able to make simple choices for themselves after being controlled for so long.

When we left the control of our parents, many of us experienced a similar relief, at least in our physical existence. We could finally make our own choices and build our lives and relationships according to our own beliefs and needs. But in the homes where strict obedience and authoritarian control prevail, awareness of needs is not promoted. We were encouraged, if not forced, to arrange our lives according to the convenience of our parents, not according to our own needs. In the authoritarian home, individual rights do not exist for children. The few rights that are recognized can be overridden at any time by the needs of the parent. For example, a slumber party that has been promised earlier can be immediately canceled if the parents have to be elsewhere. Dinner menus are arranged to convenience parental tastes. Being able to join playmates for an afternoon is contingent on parents not having other plans or demands for their children's time.

As a result, we children of past generations were relatively unfamiliar with defending our own interests, and knowing our own needs and feelings. Once we got out on our own, we had a great time just doing what we felt like. However, we never designed for ourselves any guidelines for dealing with power and control, since as children we were usually not allowed to taste it. Nor did we observe a model of power sharing. When we became parents we had no framework for our newfound power other than what we ourselves had been subjected to as children. We are therefore dragging along with us the internal bondage that was implanted in us during our childhoods. We end up forcing our children into the same repressed state we once experienced ourselves. We do this not necessarily because we believe it is right or beneficial, but because it gives us a framework for expressing the need to control, which we were deprived of during our own childhood.

This deep-rooted feeling, this suppressed need to be able to have control over our destinies, is thus passed from generation to generation. Parents repeatedly play out their own squelched desire for power by overcontrolling their children. Our inability to admit occasional failures to our children is therefore not necessarily because of pride. It is in part a refusal to relinquish the outlet for power that we were raised to believe was the inherent right of parents. Within many of us, there is a seething rage over the lack of control we had over our childhood experiences, and we keep it suppressed by suppressing our children. Unless we each get in touch with these feelings of powerlessness, we will undoubtably pave the way for the same rigid attitudes in our own children.

How do we avoid this? How do we teach obedience without setting ourselves up as authorities to be unquestioningly obeyed? More important, how do we establish an example of right and wrong if we allow our children to see that we often fall short ourselves?

The answer is considering children as being our equals, in rights, feelings, needs, and especially in the struggle to behave morally. Our authoritarian backgrounds taught us that right and wrong are within the authority figure, which is where we get the idea that we have to teach children to see us as being the authority of right and wrong. In reality, right and wrong stands by itself. Religious teachings suggest that right and wrong existed in this world long before we were here, and will still be around long after we leave. There is a standard of moral excellence to which God expects us all to adhere, parent and child alike. Of course, exactly what *is* right and wrong will vary somewhat as they play themselves out within the principles of love and justice. But we need to convey to our child that *both* generations are subject to a right and wrong that is bigger than themselves.

Children learn obedience from the model of obedience we provide. We can provide no greater model of confession and asking for forgiveness than by admitting our mistakes to our children and asking for their forgiveness. They learn that it is O.K. to be imperfect, but that imperfection often requires restitution. They learn how to make up for their errors by watching us make up for ours.

Writer Gary Smalley points out that our insensitive rigidity can lead a child to "close his spirit."[9] When parents are unfair or unfeeling, children close themselves off. Staying open to contact with parents leaves a child vulnerable, and vulnerability allows people to be hurt. Children build a wall between themselves and their parents when they see parents as an unbending source of pain. Smalley describes a five-point system that can help "reopen a child's spirit" after we have erred. This system follows the blueprint of confession and asking forgiveness. Below are synopses of his five steps:

1. Become tenderhearted. We need to show our own vulnerability. By humbling ourselves with a gentler, less severe emotional stance, we communicate the following:

    a. He is valuable and important. We express this importance in nonverbal ways. We are slow to move toward him. Our heads may be bowed down, and we are obviously grieved that we have hurt him.

    b. We do not want to see his spirit closed; we care about him.

    c. We know that there is something wrong. We acknowledge by our softness that an offense has taken place and we are going to *slow down* long enough to correct whatever has happened.

    d. We are open to listen. It is safe for him to share what has happened and we are not going to get angry or hurt him again.[10]

2. Increase your understanding. Here we attempt to find out what is going on. We clarify what actually happened from the child's standpoint. Often we walk into a situation without being aware of all the factors and motivations involved, and because of this we may jump the gun.

In addition, we try to find out what the child's feelings are as a result of what has just happened. Often children are unable to put into words just exactly how they are feeling. It is difficult for them to accurately label emotions such as hurt, anger, and depression. Smalley suggests that we try to help our children express themselves through use of comparisons, which he calls "word pictures." Expressions like "the rug has been pulled out from under me," "I feel blue," and "the roof is caving in on me" all express feelings by comparing them to something more concrete.

3. Recognize your offense. We point out that we erred. It could be that our child really did need some form of discipline, but we went about correcting him inappropriately. Perhaps we were too harsh, too unclear in what he was being corrected for, did not recognize other guilty parties, or corrected in anger instead of in reason. Being able to admit these types of errors shows us to be honorable people, worthy of respect. Exposing our imperfection also shows that we consider our child to be important enough to merit our confession.

4. Attempt to touch your child. We can access how far our

child's spirit has reopened by trying to establish some sort of physical contact. His willingness to allow us to touch him indicates that our softness, understanding, and admission of guilt have succeeded in breaking down the barrier of anger. In addition, touching in itself helps establish a bond of closeness.

5. *Seek your child's forgiveness.* We ask the child if he would be willing to forgive us. Asking for forgiveness shows the child that we cherish something that only he can give, and helps him see how special he is to us.

Imagine that you are an employee in a crowded office. Your employer comes bursting into the room and stomps up to your desk. She delivers a five-minute tirade concerning some misdeed that you know nothing about. You try to get a word in edgewise, but she is so upset she does not even notice that you are trying to set her straight. When she pauses to catch her breath, you point out your innocence. Without a word, she turns on her heel, stomps over to another employee's desk, and starts in on him. You are left feeling attacked, embarrassed, and humiliated.

Suppose again that this confrontation took place. However, this time, as you begin to defend yourself, your employer stops yelling and listens. As it becomes clear that she has erred, her head begins to bow, her facial expression softens, and the tenseness begins to leave her body. She asks questions about how the misdeed may have come about. She admits that she has been too hasty, and apologizes for the attack. She offers to shake hands and asks for forgiveness. You are left feeling perhaps a little worse for wear, but otherwise you feel closer to your boss than you did before. You believe that she is an honorable woman, and will give her the benefit of the doubt in the future. You look up to her because you place trust in her integrity.

Children react to our confrontations similarly. If we wrongly attack them they feel hurt, but it hurts even more when we make no attempt to offer restitution. They may continue to obey us out of fear, but not because they believe in us. Certainly, loving obedience is our preference, and it helps children form a useful framework for building their morals as well.

EXPLAINING MOTIVES

Children can watch us perform many moral acts. But unless they understand why we have chosen to act in a certain way, these acts may never become a part of their behavioral repertoire. Children need to know why we do what we do. This can be accomplished by disclosing our own self-reward systems. Such disclosure helps them conceive of what it is like to experience inner guidance.

For example, sometimes when we are driving we may slow down unnecessarily in order to allow another driver to enter the stream of traffic. At this point we may say, "I'm glad I slowed down to let that guy in. He was waiting there a long time. I know I would have been relieved to get in after waiting so long." We not only would be modeling empathy for the person in need, but also would be pointing out that we feel good inside for having helped. This permits children to feel good about their own altruistic behavior and to feel free to pat themselves on the back when it is appropriate.

Our motives can also be explained within the framework of moral exhortations. For the preceding example, we could add something like, "I find that it is best to consider what it is like for the other guy." This models for the child the general principle behind such behavior, which can be reapplied to a variety of situations.

Another example involves exposing an internal rationale for a certain act. When Christian parents tithe their income, rarely are the children in on the procedure. Children can learn about charity if parents take them aside and show them what they are doing when they tithe. This involves pointing out the amount of income, showing the portion of it that will go to the church and the reasons behind the chosen percentage, and saying "I feel good about giving this money to the church. The Lord is responsible for my having any income at all, and I am glad that I am able to give part of it back to be used for his work." These explanations not only give children the reasoning behind our actions, but also model the concern over helping others that is involved in charity. Ironically, a common parental method for teaching tithing is to force children to tithe their own income. Chapter 5 pointed out what a detrimental effect on future charitable acts that forcing sharing can have.

WHAT DOES COERCION MODEL?

Since children see everything we do as a potential model for their own behavior, consider what the coercive model of discipline teaches them. First, it shows a model of demanding your own way. Even though we couch our coercions with "It's for your own good" and all sorts of similar expressions, no matter what our motives, we are still modeling an example of unswerving insistence that their behaviors conform to our desires.

Second, it models the idea that when people don't do what we want them to do, we find a way to punish them. Little wonder that children fall so easily into hitting one another when they disagree. How many times have they experienced such treatment from their parents? The concept of "getting even" is not difficult to extract from observing a coercive role model.

Modeling vengefulness and demandingness is a pitfall of coercive discipline that is not easy to avoid, other than by not using coercion whenever possible. Admitting our errors in discipline, as described earlier, is one act that may help show flexibility rather than demandingness. But vengefulness poses a more difficult problem, especially since we are usually angry when we find the need to punish. And even if we delivered punishment like emotionless automatons, the idea of hurting another person because that person has not done as we see fit is still unchallenged. This is one issue I will have to leave for future researchers to wrestle with.

EMPATHY TRAINING

As was pointed out in chapter 3, children have a natural capacity for empathy. Without any encouragement at all from parents, they will feel uncomfortable around others in distress. If they can find a solution that will alleviate the mutual anxiety, altruism will be reinforced. The child will repeat the altruistic act because he has learned that it will relieve the discomfort his empathy arouses. We can instruct children on *how* to go about helping others through the pretending games we play with them.

Children frequently play games where the participants act out certain roles. When the parent is included in the game, she can model various empathic and altruistic attitudes. For example, if the children are playing Super Eagle and Kluck Kent can't find a phone booth to change in, the parent could say something like, "Oh, poor Kluck Kent, you must be upset that you can't find a phone booth. I know! You can come and change over here." Within the constraints of the game, the parent could have modeled empathy and shown how a solution could be found to provide relief from the distress.

Studies have shown that role-playing concerning the theme of helping another in distress has more of an effect on girls, and boys are affected more by role-playing concerning the theme of sharing.[11] Why this difference exists is not entirely certain. Perhaps girls respond to the needs for help because of identification with the stereotypical nurturant-mother role, and boys are identifying with the stereotypical provider-father role and are sharing accordingly. Whatever the reason for this difference, role-playing games are influential in increasing altruism in either sex.

Younger children also play imaginative games with dolls, puppets, "superhero" figures, and so forth. When we take the time to get down on the floor with our children and become part of the games, unlimited moral lessons can be demonstrated. For example, in a popular children's-toy game where wooden figures are driving around in their wooden cars, we might say, "Uh-oh, Mr. Smith ran out of gas. He is just stuck there. How sad he is! Here comes Mr. Jones. It makes him sad to see that Mr. Smith ran out of gas and is not able to go anywhere. Look, Mr. Jones is giving Mr. Smith some of his gas. Now they can both drive around. They are all so happy now." We again would be modeling both empathy and a solution that alleviates the bad feelings. Research has shown that such games are indeed likely to increase altruistic behavior.[12]

CONCLUSION

Children pattern their behavior after those whom they admire. In order for altruism to be a part of their socialization, it must be evident in the children's role models. Examining the visibility of our own altruistic behavior helps us reassess how we react to others in our children's presence. Unfortunately, not even moral exhortation can counteract a behavioral pattern set in motion by modeling. Therefore, it is crucial that we take seriously what kind of example we are setting.

EXERCISES

1. List three things you do in front of your children that you would like to stop doing, or at least alter.
2. List three things you would like to start doing or making more visible to your children.
3. In the following situations, write how you would explain to your children why you are doing what you are doing, both with regard to rationale and empathy (see page 138 for sample responses).
   a. A man with a white cane is standing out in the middle of the street, struggling to figure out where the curb is. You go out into the intersection and help him to the curb.
   b. A neighbor girl falls and skins her knee. You go put your arm around her and comfort her.
   c. A woman from your church goes into the hospital and her husband and children are at home fending for themselves. You fix a casserole and take it over for them.
4. Write a monologue, such as the ones on page 138, to be used while playing with your child's favorite toys; illustrate these themes:
   a. one character defending another.
   b. one character sharing with another.
   c. one character comforting another.

CHAPTER SEVEN

At What Age?

The preceding chapters have touched on many different techniques of intervention for encouraging internalization. However, we have spent very little time looking at which interventions work better at which ages. What works well at one age may not work well at all at another age. For example, giving detailed explanations of why God venerates justice will bounce right off a three-year-old. Likewise, if a group of young teenagers are rude to someone and you go into a melodramatic display of emotion over the feelings of the victim of the rudeness, you will most likely be laughed right out of the room. Tempering interventions according to the receptive abilities of the child's age group ensures that some good will be accomplished.

In the same way as through the moral stages discussed earlier, children also pass through a number of socially based stages as they grow and learn.[1] At each of these social stages, the child is faced with a different developmental task. In order to successfully pass through the various stages, children make decisions about themselves that affect their future ego functioning. For example, an infant's developmental task involves either learning to trust, or deciding that people are basically untrustworthy. Successfully resolving this stage— deciding to trust—results in the child's ability to hope.

Other stages children pass through involve the development of their thinking skills, or how they perceive and make sense of their world.[2] For example, the young infant is unable to perceive objects as being permanent. If an object or person is outside the infant's view, he assumes that the entity no longer exists. This is one reason infants often go through a stage of crying hysterically when their mothers leave them for brief periods: They assume that because Mother is not visible, she is gone forever. Around the age of ten months, the child understands that objects and people exist whether or not they are currently in view, and he can more easily tolerate his mother's absence.

How we handle our children can affect how easily they pass through each social stage. The infant's decision to endorse the trustworthiness of others is shaped by the trustworthiness of his caretaker. If his caretaker is unreliable in providing basic needs such as food, comfort, and affection, the child is likely to become frustrated and demanding. Such characteristics may endure indefinitely if the child is never given opportunity to discover that others are willing to meet his needs without his being demanding and obnoxious.

The child's thinking abilities are also important to remember as we react to him. Becoming frustrated, angry, and impatient with the hysterical infant who has not yet learned object permanence is punitive and unfair, and is experienced by the child as even further rejection or desertion. Likewise, never allowing the infant to have time away from mother restricts both his opportunities for learning that she will come back, and his skills at comforting himself when he is upset.

So it appears that parents have tasks of their own as their children pass through stages. As a child wrestles with each developmental task, his parents have a complementary task of encouraging as well as avoiding hindrance of its progress.

The type of discipline we use with children must also take into account their developmental tasks. Additionally, disciplines we choose should not be fraught with expectations that go beyond the child's reasoning ability. The remainder of this chapter will not only describe how well various moral interventions work at each age, but will also take into account both the child's and the parent's developmental tasks.

Children can begin to move away from the "if it feels good, it must be right" type of morality at around the age of eighteen months. Therefore, the following age groups are discussed:

ages 1½–3, ages 3–6, ages 6–12, and teenagers. These age boundaries are not absolute: Some children are capable of advanced reasoning at a very young age; other children are slower in their development. You can use your own observations and judgment to decide which stage your child's behavior most closely resembles. We will look at the most effective interventions, which include inner labeling, acceptance of offers of altruism, reasoning, moral exhortation, and modeling. I will not describe specific issues that tend to occur with each age group. For those who are interested in such a discussion, I recommend Schulman and Mekler's *Bringing Up a Moral Child.*[3]

EIGHTEEN MONTHS TO THREE YEARS

This stage is the transition period between babyhood and childhood. On the outside, the child has become more mobile, more independent, and better at communicating with others. But on the inside he is still the infant, demanding that his needs be met, and not very skilled in a socialized way at negotiating need fulfillment.

Temper tantrums are one product of this inability to compromise. The child knows what he wants, he's not getting it, and there's nothing left for him to do but let loose his marginally controllable inner rage.

Of course, what is happening in his social environment will influence how well he pulls through the tantrum stage. If parents give in to his wishes when he throws a tantrum, he will learn that throwing tantrums is a means of getting one's way. We all know adults who have never progressed past this stage and still bully others with their anger, rather than work out conflict in a more agreeable manner. On the other hand, becoming punitive for temper tantrums would be the equivalent of punishing children for their immaturity, ultimately resulting in a low evaluation of themselves owing to their implied "badness." The parent's task then, is to react in ways that avoid rewarding tantrums, and also teach the child other ways of getting his needs communicated and met.

The best way to react to a temper tantrum is to ignore it,

perhaps even to walk away from the child if the din is ear-shattering. Some children will follow a parent who is trying to walk away from tantrum behavior, in hope that she will respond more compliantly. Although some parents might try to make their child stay in his room until the tantrum is over, it might be easier for the parent to lock herself away in her room until it's over.

With time, the child will learn that temper tantrums are not as likely to get him what he wants as more socialized interactions will, and he will also develop skills at comforting his inner rage when he must put his needs and demands on hold.

Once the tantrum ends, offering affection and acceptance—and perhaps even discussing what happened, with children closer to age three—teaches the child that he is still loved, and that there are other ways of communicating needs. It is also vitally important that we listen to and work with our children's early efforts to make requests and negotiate needs. As with any intervention, ignoring tantrum behavior should not be taken to the extreme, where every time a child expresses an unpleasant emotion, he experiences love withdrawal by his parents.

Temper tantrum situations are also a product of a child's learning about his separateness. The child has learned from experience that mother is indeed an entity separate from his will, and that she can either satisfy or frustrate needs. This emphasizes the separateness of his will. With guidance he will learn how to experience and make use of his will in an autonomous manner that is comfortable for both himself and others.

Overcoercion at this age annihilates the child's ability to provide self-direction, yet overpermissiveness does not give the child feedback concerning how far he can go and still get along with people. If parents are either too permissive or too coercive and punitive, the child eventually experiences shame and doubt, rather than feelings of autonomy and self-control.

The major task of a child in this age group, then, is to develop a clear sense of being an autonomously driven individual, which is experienced both socially and personally as a positive state of being. And the major task of parenting this age group is to find a healthful balance between allowing autonomy and teaching the child how far his rights to autonomy can be extended.

Inner labeling. Inner labeling does not appear to have any greater effect on this age group than does positive reinforcement in the form of praise. The distinction between "good thing to do" and "good me" is apparently still too fine for the very young to comprehend, so they interpret all positive statements as they would interpret praise. However, we are still better off to attempt to state praise in the form of inner labeling just for the sake of forming the good habit of using it, since when our children are older it will become more effective than praise. For the very young, an inner label needs to be kept simple, such as saying "good boy," so that it does not exceed their verbal abilities.

Acceptance of offers of altruism. A child this young is likely to make only a limited number of realistic offers to help. Usually when he does offer, it is because he has seen someone else do the task before and it looks as though it might be fun, or might make the child feel important. At this age the child does not recognize the selfish aspect of the offer, since he is still in the process of graduating from the completely self-preserving standpoint of infancy. To him, selfishness is a way of life! In order to help the child move away from selfishness and focus more on his empathic self, he would benefit not only from our accepting his offers whenever possible, but also from our showing how happy we are when he helps. The happy tone of voice, big smile, and grateful expression on a parent's face make a greater impression on the very young child than the actual words "good boy!" or "thank you!" which we might use. Such reactions to a child's helpfulness guide him away from his selfish motives and help him realize how good he feels when he helps others. Likewise, they reinforce a productive way to assert his will.

Reasoning. As we consider the limited verbal ability of this age group, note that reasoning works better when emphasized emotionally, rather than cognitively. For example, if a two-year-old pushes over another child, a parent might say, "You hurt Bobby; he's crying." An emotional delivery of this observation, which includes a sad face and pained tone of voice mimicking the feelings of the injured boy, will connect much more quickly. The very young often do not fully understand how their actions affect others unless the effect is pointed out to them. When we explain the effect emotionally, the child's cognitive restraints are bypassed and he is put in touch with his empathic self.

Moral exhortation. Saying no to a two-year-old is like waving a red flag in front of a bull. Telling him not to do something is a guarantee that he's going to charge into the forbidden behavior at the very next opportunity. This is one way the child reassures himself that his will is separate. However, if the "no" as a reasoning intervention is emotionally expanded, the oppositional reaction can be partially avoided. In the case mentioned above, a parent might emotionally say, "Don't push people, they can get hurt and that would make them cry," again, with the empathized pain apparent in the parent's voice. As we saw in chapter 5, simply stating this exhortation without the use of emotion will actually increase the occurrence of the undesired behavior. It seems that at times we need to become actors to survive the terrible twos!

Modeling. The very young do not think through the broader implications of the behaviors that are modeled in front of them. The world is a new place for them, and they are still learning the rudiments of appropriate behavior. This limits the behaviors they choose to copy to ones that are generally in action only, with little rationale for doing them other than to see what happens. This is a means for children to exercise and learn about their will. One common parental behavior two-year-olds frequently copy is yelling no. The tone of voice a parent uses is another prime modeling influence. Little things like picking up items that have fallen to the ground, wiping up messes, and placing things in cabinets or garbage cans (with the difference not always being recognized) are also likely to be copied. How a parent handles anger is an important influence at this age: When the child misbehaves, does the parent strike the child in anger? If she does, the child learns that when you are angry at people, you hit them. All of these modeling examples involve learning day-to-day basic behavior rules, at which the child is still getting his firsthand experience. Exposure to deeper interpretations, such as explaining to a child the motive for doing a certain thing, is of limited worth.

THREE YEARS TO SIX YEARS

By age three, the child has begun to explore what roles he might fill in the world. He has discovered his imaginative and creative abilities, and has begun to play-act various social positions, both real and fantasized. He becomes questioning and intrusive, and in this manner discovers the boundaries of his social roles.

Successfully passing through this stage results in a sense of purpose. The child will feel comfortable in taking the initiative to pursue goals, because he knows he has the capacity to learn and succeed within his individual role. Difficulties arise when parents are not accepting of their child's individual efforts. Overzealous efforts to cram children into preconceived molds work against the development of initiative, and instead produce feelings of guilt over what the child perceives as inappropriate assertion and therefore evidence of his "badness." For example, if a child shows interest in playing with dolls and stuffed animals, and his parents discourage such pastimes and push him toward the erector set, the child will question his ability to choose what feels right for him. The key parenting task for this age group is demonstrating acceptance and willingness to tolerate exploratory social behavior.

Children's reasoning skills during this stage are more recognizable by what they cannot accomplish than by what they are capable of. They have much difficulty taking into account more than one line of reasoning at once. Their egocentrism, which does not let them see outside their own perspective, is also limiting. A child may point into a field of pretty flowers and say, "See that pretty flower, Mommy," without awareness that mother would not be able to see inside his head and know which flower he meant. Although this can at times seem self-centered or selfish, it is not. Recognizing perspectives other than one's own comes with learning, just as any other process is learned from or shaped by the environment. Over time, careful explanations and patience with the child's limitations will increase his sphere of recognized perspectives. Obviously, criticizing or penalizing him for such natural limitations is inappropriate.

Inner labeling. Since preschoolers are in the process of defining their roles, inner labels are helpful in defining the characteristics of those roles, such as being a good helper, a caring person, and so on. The effectiveness of inner labeling over praise does not come into play until the child is approaching age six, so for the most part, either intervention can help the preschooler see his role in a positive, productive light. Likewise, negative labeling can result in his viewing his role as being undesirable. And since he still has difficulty seeing the difference between "bad boy" and "bad thing to do," he can even view criticism as a reflection of who he is. Experiencing parental approval is therefore a very important part of the preschooler's development.

Acceptance of offers of altruism. Preschoolers become aware of what needs to be done and when, and can therefore start making more realistic offers than were possible when they were younger. This is the time for parents to begin capitalizing on these offers by finding some way that the child can help out when he shows the willingness to do so. Accepting his offers helps him define his social roles. Again, appreciativeness shown for services rendered will help the child realize that it feels good to help others.

Reasoning. As preschoolers develop they begin to make use of their growing ability to reason, rather than their emotions. Therefore, parents can begin to put more emphasis on the rationales behind choosing or not choosing certain behaviors. Making reference to how it would feel if the child were the victim, or what some respected other person would do in a similar circumstance are good possibilities. However, an emotional delivery should still be used, since it presents to the child an example of the results of his behavior and thus allows him to store the experience in his memory in both a cognitive and an emotional way.

Moral exhortation. Preschoolers are very good at latching on to rules. Life is much more simple and secure if there are absolute rules to live it by, and accepting the rules laid down by others builds this security for young children. This does not mean they will not test authority figures to find out how much they can get away with; the issue is that they do not question whether the rules they are rebelling against are valid or changeable. Because of this, moral exhortation is a valuable intervention for this age. It is important that the rules that get to the child first come from parents, teachers, and other responsible authority figures, rather than from other children, who may or may not have their facts straight. Moral exhortations can be useful for this age group not only after a transgression, but also whenever else they can be rationally squeezed into daily interactions.

Modeling. Implied rules can be just as influential on the behavior of this age group as stated rules. Preschoolers become aware of how people tend to treat one another and will assume that it is appropriate for them to use those same mannerisms themselves. They are particularly interested in the activities of same-sex role models. As we saw in chapter 5, if a modeled behavior is not the same as an exhorted behavior, the modeled behavior will be followed. When our children reach this age, we should begin to be particularly aware of whether we practice what we preach. When our own behavior in our child's presence has missed the mark, we can teach our morals by pointing out that we have indeed erred and will try to do better in the future. Fantasy and creative play are commonplace and flexible at this age, which makes it a prime time for empathy training through games as well.

SIX YEARS TO TWELVE YEARS

By the time children reach this stage, their interests have begun to swing away from home and into the direction of school. Their new primary task is to develop a sense of competence. Feelings of competence come about as children learn the new skills, ideas, and activities that will ultimately prepare them for their futures. Successfully completing this phase results in feelings of "industry," or the ability to accomplish. Failure or perceived failure to be able to perform tasks independently results in feelings of inferiority.

The parent's task is to help the child view his efforts as successful. The child will not view his efforts as successful if every time he shows his parents his latest accomplishments or creations, he gets the reaction, "That's good, but this and this and that are wrong with it." When possible, limit comments to what is praiseworthy about a child's efforts. If he expresses displeasure or frustration over some aspect, ask if he would like some advice before you bombard him with suggestions. If you see something grotesquely deficient, create an opportunity for needed instruction at a later date, but not during the time he has chosen to seek validation of his efforts through your approval.

Another parental task for children of this age group is rule provision. These children become seemingly bottomless repositories for all pieces of information that help them understand why the world works the way it does. They will not be satisfied with your stating what the rules are; they will also demand a detailed explanation of *why* such a rule came to be. Although they still have difficulty with complex thinking skills, such as thinking by way of hypotheses needing to be tested rather than being absolute truths, they can still think logically and systematically, as long as explanations involve concrete situations. They are not able to think of all possible solutions to a problem; they may try more than one but then give up. The concept of rules being changeable will also be difficult for them to handle, until the latter part of this age span. The more pieces of information we provide, and the more we explain the reasoning behind a rule—thus making it potentially changeable—the easier it will be for our children to successfully complete this stage.

Inner labeling. During these years, inner labeling has its greatest effectiveness. The child knows himself to be a separately functioning individual who is being recognized and labeled for his own abilities and characteristics. This prime time lasts until around age ten, when praise and inner labels again become interchangeable in effectiveness owing to the child's increased cognitive ability.

Inner labeling can be less direct at this age and the child will still interpret it well. For example, instead of telling a child he is a sharing person, a parent may say, "You must feel really good inside knowing that you made Johnny happy when you shared." A younger child might have difficulty sorting out all the concepts referred to in such a complex inner description; however, the six-year-olds through twelve-year-olds have developed the thinking skills necessary to be aware of such progressions of feelings and events. Awareness of such progressions allows the child to recognize his own good feelings about helping others, and validates his belief in his skills as being competent.

Acceptance of offers of altruism. Children in this age group have adjusted for the most part to family life and their place in it, which includes using a number of social and practical living skills. Accepting offers to help is therefore not only beneficial for their moral development, but also is an important part of their getting practice with new skills. We need to make sure that we do not insult a child's abilities at this age. For example, if the child offers to help with the laundry he may feel that he is being put off or is unneeded if his mother hands him a folded towel to place on the top of the stack. Children at this age need to have more challenging tasks than they did when they were younger, in order to still feel as if they are accomplishing something worthwhile. Likewise, the task must not be too difficult for them, such as requiring a seven-year-old to sort, fold, and put away an entire load of laundry completely on his own. Failing at a task can also result in feelings of inadequacy.

Reasoning. Because of their focus on learning about the world, children of this age are very receptive to reasoning. They may balk after being told of how something they did affected another negatively, which can leave us wondering whether or not our efforts are worth the bother. However, if we stay alert, we may later overhear our child emphatically sharing the same reasoning with a friend when the friend transgresses. Again, parenting sometimes takes a lot of tolerance for delay of seeing visible results!

Moral exhortation. Moral exhortations are still a good method of driving a point home. However, be prepared to provide plenty of explanations *why* the exhortation is true. Children of this age are not just trying to wriggle out of a sticky situation when they repeatedly ask, But why? They genuinely want to know how the rules of their world are put together and rationalized. The why's at this age are generally more important than the actual exhortation.

Modeling. Another way children learn about functioning with complex social skills is by watching how others use them. Here is where positive attitudes toward authority and restricting aggression toward others can be demonstrated for maximum benefit, since the child's receptiveness is at its peak. Not only should the behaviors and attitudes be made visible to the child, they should also be followed by an explanation of the parents' motivations for doing what they have done.

TEENAGERS

Despite the romanticizing of adolescence by the media, the teen years can be a miserable time of life. The teen must endure gross hormonal changes, an increasingly changed body, a completely confused identity, wild swings of emotions, and little certainty about where his future may lead him.[4] Imagine how we would feel if we were suddenly subjected to such a state of affairs—and with no adult-life experience to guide us! It is little wonder that teens have such a difficult time, and in turn make life difficult for their parents. It is also a scary time for parents, since many rebellious behaviors can have tragic, long-term consequences.

There are many how-to books that deal with how to control teenagers. Unfortunately, the advice they give is usually oversimplified, works with only a small number of teenagers part of the time, and is often misapplied by parents.[5]

Parents who try to find ways to prevent adolescence are fighting a lost cause. The rebellion of the teen years is a developmental stage necessary for people to find their identities. Parents have their chance for influencing their child in earlier years; by the time the child reaches his teens he pretty much knows what his parents believe and what is expected of him. Trying to have the same sort of influence over his actions as was possible when he was younger is unrealistic anyway, since teenagers are bigger, smarter, more independent, and more mobile.[6] Parents need to set house rules, set up realistic consequences for breaking them, and leave the rest of control over the child's behavior to the discretion of the inner principles the parent has encouraged throughout the teenager's childhood.

As long as the lines of communication are kept open, teens will feel free to look for their parents' advice when they need it.

Christian parents often feel that rebellion is "sin" no matter what the age of the child. What these parents have failed to take into account is that even Jesus as a twelve-year-old had his parents worried sick by taking off for three days to study at the temple courts without informing them (see Luke 2:41-52). If Jesus led a life without sin, how then can teenage rebellion be considered "sinful"?

Docile, overcontrolled teens will either experience adolescence after they leave home, or wait until their middle years and have a devastating mid-life crisis. We all need to know who we are in order to know what we have to offer our world. The rebellion of adolescence is necessary to seek out this knowledge. The parents' task during this stage is to allow teenagers to break away, and not unduly restrict or feed the rebellion.

Inner labeling. One might guess that this developmental stage would be a great time to pour on the inner labels, since there is such a heavy focus on identity. But teenagers are a completely different breed from children of other ages. They try to solve their developmental task by removing themselves as far as possible from the parents' beliefs, thereby knowing for sure that they are indeed functioning on the basis of a separate identity. They often look to their peer group for their standards, rather than to parents, teachers, and other authority figures.

For this reason, any inner label applied by parents or other authorities would at best be indirect, since the teen can be relied on to do the opposite of the label. A direct statement like "you must be a very caring person" guarantees that the teenager will act in an unhelpful manner in the future, just to prove that he is indeed his own person. Indirect statements, such as "you must feel proud," or "that must feel good" refer to the child's feelings rather than to who he is, and are less threatening to his striving for identity. Even smiling, patting him on the back, and saying "all right!" after an altruistic act helps put him in touch with his empathy without overemphasizing that the parent has him pegged.

Acceptance of offers of altruism. Spontaneous offers of altruism from many teenagers may come few and far between. When they do come and are accepted, the focus should be on how the parent or other helped person feels after having been helped. The extreme emotional theatrics, which were helpful with the younger child, are not appropriate with this age group. If a teenager, especially an early adolescent, thinks his mother is being phony, he will either call her on it or walk away, groaning "Give me a break!" A simple "Thanks, I appreciate that," much the same as we might say to our peers, avoids an appearance of insincerity.

As part of fighting the identity influenced by his parents, a teen may offer to do something completely different from the expectations his parents have for him. For example, a teenage girl may ask to be adequately instructed to be able to change the oil in the car. A teenage boy may show an interest in making quiche. Accepting offers such as these and giving the instruction necessary to be able to follow through on them not only teaches the teen new skills, but also lets him know that the parent is not standing in the way of his striving for an identity, which in turn can loosen up some of his oppositional attitudes toward his parents.

Reasoning. Reasoning for this age group needs to be as nonjudgmental and nonauthoritarian as possible, so it will not be seen as a parental belief to be rebelled against. Rationales presented as absolute, such as "Your talking during the church service ruined the message for the entire congregation" implies the parental position to be rebelled against. Stating it less rigidly, such as "It's my impression that some of the parishioners had a hard time hearing while you were talking during the service—it was probably frustrating for them," sounds less like a parental must and more like the statement of an observation, perhaps worthy enough to listen to. Other beginnings for nonjudgmental rationales are "It's my understanding that . . ."; "The way I've heard it is . . ."; "Some people have thought that . . ."; "One way of looking at this is . . ."; and so on.

Moral exhortation. Moral exhortation should be thrown out the window during adolescence. The more a parent exhorts, the more the teenager will rebel, since doing what his parents believe is right is perceived as a threat to his identity. This does not mean that parents do not say which behaviors will or will not be allowed under their roofs. It means that instead of telling the child that a certain behavior is what *should* or *should not* be done, the child should be told *why* a certain rule has been adopted for the household. Rather than telling the child "You should never play the stereo that loud—it blasts your eardrums, drives us up the wall, and ticks off the neighbors as well," he could be told "The house rule is that the stereo cannot be turned up that loud—we chose this rule because it takes into account the feelings of those who do not want to listen to the stereo."

Modeling. Modeling is important for teens, since they often structure their quest for identity around the characteristics of an idol, such as a rock singer, movie star, or other public figure. Eventually their ideal models become more realistic, such as teachers, pastors, friends' parents, coaches, or other youth-group workers. When a teen makes it clear that he admires someone who is a good model (or even just says something good about someone who would be a good influence), we can encourage him by casually saying things like "Yeah, I think I can see how he's good at helping you guys out"; "You know, I think you're right—she does have a good sense of humor"; "Wow, it sounds as if she really did do a nice job of showing you how to do that"; and so on. So long as we do not sound coercively enthusiastic, this approach can help the teenager feel free and confident in his choice of identity ideals, and less encouraged to be rebellious. Of course, all teenagers are different, and they will differ in their sensitivity to parental absolutes. You can use your own judgment concerning how important it is with your teen to avoid displaying an absolute to be rebelled against.

Teenagers are so focused on how they fit into an identity that they are masters at recognizing when our actions do not fit in with our purported identity. Teenagers not only recognize hypocrisy but will be likely to point it out to us when they see it. If we swallow our defensiveness during such confrontations and admit our error, wherever it may lie, teenagers will have an excellent model for being true to whatever identity they eventually settle into.

CHAPTER EIGHT

Lying

Thus far, we have been establishing a philosophy of how to bring about moral learning. How to deal with specific moral transgressions has been mentioned only in passing. It is beyond the scope of this book to examine every moral mistake a child might make. However, there are numerous considerations we have touched on that must be taken into account when we are deciding how to react to our child's misbehavior. For the purpose of providing an example, I have chosen to elaborate how this is done using the example of lying.

Lying is such a disturbing subject for parents that I feel it deserves a special chapter. It is a shortcoming that is particularly embarrassing for parents when it appears, especially since young children's "lying" is usually transparent to those who witness it. Parents are to be commended when they do place a high priority on honesty. Without it, a child's ability to be trustworthy or responsible would always be in question. However, the issue of lying is more complex than first meets the eye. Without taking into account the intricate details, we could deliver consequences for lying based on outward appearances and feelings of embarrassment or frustration. Even with the best intentions we could use interventions that are ineffective, unfair, or even detrimental to the training of honesty. This chapter will look at lying as a developmental phenomenon, and will suggest ways of handling dishonesty that will not punish children just for being children.

One form of lying in very young children (ages 3–5) stems from their need to feel separate from mother. Until that time, they believe that mother can see the thoughts inside their heads. One way of challenging this belief is to tell mother something that is not true, just to see if mother can look into their heads and recognize what really happened. These "lies" can be quite unsophisticated, such as saying "Johnny has a pet alligator under his bed." It is important that these stories go unchallenged. If mother says "that's ridiculous," the child interprets the response as meaning that mother sees the truth by reading his thoughts. This reaction squelches the normal separating and forming of an identity of his own. Furthermore, it may result in more stories of this sort until he can affirm his separateness. A more appropriate response might be, "Oh, really? How exciting!" and allowing the child to elaborate on his newfound individual story-telling ability.

Another issue that contributes to lying involves children's abilities at different ages. In chapter 7, we looked at the various skills children have at certain times. The area of cognitive development most relevant to lying is illustrated by the following incident.

When Bridie was about four, she asked me where she could find her pajamas. "They're in the dryer," I told her, and she padded off to the laundry room. Shortly thereafter she came running back, announcing, "They're not in the dryer. They're in the wetter!"

This one-track-mind thinking involves scientific reasoning. Scientific reasoning can be described as how children process information. They take in the facts, decide which are important in making a decision, and choose or predict accordingly. These thought processes play a major role in the events leading up to the reporting of a falsehood.

The most famous example of this type of reasoning was demonstrated by Piaget's *conservation* experiments. Anyone with access to a four-year-old or five-year-old can perform this simple experiment and get consistent results. First, fill two glasses of equal size with an equal amount of water. Ask the child which glass is fuller, and most likely the child will say they are the same. If he says they are not the same, have him add or subtract water until he believes they are equal. Second, pour the contents of one of the glasses into a wide, shallow bowl. Again, ask the child which container, in this case the bowl or the glass, has the most water in it. All but the most precocious of children will say something to the effect that the bowl is fuller because the water surface is wider, or that the glass is fuller because the water level is higher. The fact that the child had proclaimed the two portions to be equivalent only seconds before is irrelevant to his decision.

The explanation for this common reasoning error of young children involves the necessity of thinking about more than one dimension. In the preceding experiment, a child would have to take into account a change in depth, width, and height to be able to *conserve,* or intellectually maintain, the amount of liquid in the containers. In the case of Bridie and the "dryer-wetter," she would have had to move to a different dimension—wash-soil—in order to be able to think of the term that actually describes the washing machine's purpose.

Unfortunately, young children are not intellectually equipped to take into account more than one dimension at a time in decision making. In the conservation experiment, this is illustrated by children's tendency to make their judgments according to width or depth alone, whichever stood out more to them, rather than all of the dimensions. According to the child's reasoning scheme, he has actually reasoned correctly: When he takes into consideration depth or width alone, the two amounts of water are indeed different, even if such a difference has no basis in adult reality. The child has made the most accurate prediction or choice he is capable of even though he is wrong. The ability to take into account more than one factor will begin around the age of seven, and will usually be solidified into many areas of reasoning by age ten.

Situations where a child chooses to lie also involve a large number of relevant variables to sort out. For example, in the case of a child losing his mittens, many different feelings and perceived consequences travel down the cognitive road to his decision-destination of how to report the loss to his mother. The following thoughts illustrate their diversity:

"Those were my favorite mittens; I'm sad that I lost them."
"Johnny knows I lost them and might tell on me."

"They might still be at school somewhere."
"Mom says I should always tell the truth."
"Mom might buy me a new pair if I tell her about it."
"My hands will be cold without those mittens."
"If I tell Mom about it, I might get punished."

Recall that a young child does not take into account all of these related issues when deciding what to say; he chooses the issue that stands out the most to him and bases his decision on that. By scanning the list above it is not difficult to guess which issue has the most familiar, ominous ring to a young child: the possibility of punishment. Therefore, his response will focus on whatever will avoid that consequence. Even though he knows that honesty is important, that Johnny will probably inform on him, and that the mittens' nonaccountability will eventually become obvious, he will lie about their whereabouts because the threat of punishment overrides all other important factors.

Years ago there was a toy commercial on television in which a mother was standing over a demolished doll house and was asking her three-year-old, "Suzie, what on earth happened to this doll house?" The commercial then showed Suzie looking up at her mother, innocently batting her big brown eyes, and replying, "nothing." In spite of the obviousness that something had indeed happened to the doll house, the biggest issue in Suzie's mind was how to avoid punishment, and she reacted accordingly. Most parents can easily report a number of occasions on which their children have made equally seemingly ridiculous assertions.

Reasoning processes are not alone in their contribution to lying. A second issue is well illustrated by a situation involving my forementioned son Ben. He and two of his cronies got carried away during one of their bike rides and traveled far beyond their acceptable boundaries. His friends eventually confessed the transgression to their parents, which resulted in my being informed of what had happened. When confronted with the evidence, Ben would not admit to any wrongdoing. When asked where he had gone, he gave vague "over there" or "around" responses, and would not admit to the more incriminating specifics of their travels. Eventually his father and I gave up trying to dredge a confession and informed him of the punishment he would receive.

However, I was still disturbed that he was so unwilling to admit to what he had done, in the face of so much incriminating evidence. Finally, I told Ben, "Look. I would really like to know where you went today. Your punishment will stay the same; I just want to hear about what happened from you." After I reaffirmed that his punishment would not be increased, he freely and in vivid detail presented a review of where they had gone. After thanking him for telling me the truth, I asked him why he had been so afraid to tell us. As it turned out, he was generalizing this situation to another that had been going on at the time. A couple of rowdies from down the road had infiltrated Ben's playing territory, and there had been frequent altercations while Ben was playing with them. We had told Ben that if there were any more problems with these boys, he would no longer be allowed to play with them. Ben had generalized this threat to include getting into trouble with his other friends, and was afraid that if we found out what they had done, he would no longer be able to play with his two best friends.

The issue illustrated above is that of extreme punishment. When punishment is too severe, children will usually lie to avoid it no matter how advanced their reasoning ability is. Ironically, parents often save severe punishment such as spanking and washing out a child's mouth with soap for lying alone, since parents consider honesty to be so important. Unfortunately, the fear of such punishments generalizes to other situations, and can actually increase children's lying as they try to avoid the possibility of severe punishments.

Although apparent lying does not approach becoming cold-blooded deception until around the age of ten, this does not mean that no consequences should be administered for saying something that is not true. Without such consequences, a child may assume that lying is an acceptable behavior, which is the feared result motivating our usual overboard reactions to lying. Instead, the consequences should be an adjunct to the more appropriate punishment the child may have been trying to avoid. For example, in the case of Ben and the Broken Bike Boundaries, Ben was restricted from using his bike for one week for breaking the rule, and lost a few additional days for not telling the truth about it. The child who lied about losing his mittens might be disciplined by losing one day of playing in the snow for being careless, and a second day for not being honest. In both cases, a punishment related to and appropriate for the original crime is given, then extended for the additional transgression of dishonesty. Let me re-emphasize, however, that "lies" which are actually a product of a child's fantasy life can be left unchallenged.

In some cases, children will lie about something when they would not have gotten into trouble in the first place, such as in the case of an accident over which the child had little or no control. For example, a child might accidentally knock over and break mom's favorite vase, then lie in order to avoid any consequences. When this happens, we can make use of the "honesty is the best policy" exhortation, since when he does start taking into account all variables he will need that bit of information to make decisions correctly. Not punishing under these circumstances also shows the child that we are sympathetic, forgiving, and reasonable, rather than merciless ogres who search for excuses to punish little children.

Fear of extreme punishment is not the only fear that motivates children to lie. They may invent stories to win parental approval, or withhold information because they are concerned that their parent will not love them because of it. In either case, the dishonesty involved is still a protective device, rather than true lying, and should be interpreted by parents as such. Parents can reduce the number of lies of this sort by reassuring their children of their love for them no matter what their successes or failures may be. This is a continuing process, not necessarily something to be relied on at the time of the falsehood.

CHRISTIAN CHILDREN ARE BIGGER LIARS?

A recent study showed that religious children score higher on a test measuring dishonesty than nonreligious children.[1] How on earth can that be? shocked Christian parents surely must ask. Christian parents generally emphasize their values much more fervently than nonreligious parents. How is it that Christian children are actually falling short in comparison to the rest of society?

Part of the explanation for these results may be because religious parents could be more likely than nonreligious parents to use the overboard punishments, since honesty is so important to them. However, I suspect that two other major phenomena are responsible for this outcome. Lie scales capitalize on two personality characteristics: the inability to admit to the normal human inadequacies to which we all fall victim from time to time, and simpleminded thinking. Christian parents, therefore, need to examine what they are doing that may encourage these two characteristics.

Christian children's difficulty with admitting error is not difficult to interpret from the actions of their parents. High standards are set for Christian children, and anything that falls short of those standards is labeled as being unacceptable to God. Therefore, Christian children are likely to lie in order to be able to describe themselves as meeting God's standard and to be "acceptable" to him and society, not to mention to be able to meet parental approval.

An error being made by Christian parents in these circumstances is related to giving children only a partial message in their spiritual training. Yes, God has high standards toward which he expects us to aim. However, he never intended that we should be able to meet them completely. He sent his Son solely for this purpose: He knows that we will fail from time to time, and being the loving God he is, he provided a means of cleansing through the Redeemer. Children need to know about this expectation God has for them; likewise, parents need to be wary that their expectations for their children are not higher than those of their Lord's. Reducing unrealistic expectations can reduce this brand of lying.

The characteristic of simplemindedness is even less pleasant for Christian parents to have to consider. Are you saying we are training our children to be less than intelligent? they might ask.

Unfortunately, Christian parents can unwittingly aim their children in that direction. Because of their fervor to let their children know that God is responsible for all creation and all valid rules of society, children can fall victim to explaining everything solely along the lines of "because God made it that way." Going no further than that to explain our complex world is indeed simpleminded.

What parents need to explain to children is *why* God made things a certain way. For example, as a child enters adolescence he usually wonders what to do with his sexuality. Scripture gives guidelines in this area by prohibiting nonmarital sex, and Christian parents usually relay this fact to their children. However, they would be helping their children solidify the concept by pointing out that such a prohibition is the result of living in an imperfect world. Indiscriminant sexual activity can result in unwanted pregnancies, unwanted marriages, abortions, neglected and unwanted children, emotional problems, transmission of a host of various diseases, and other assorted worldly miseries. Since he is a loving God, the Lord instructs us not to be promiscuous in order to protect us from harm; he does not want to see us hurt. Giving a child this sort of explanation not only gives him a strong basis for his eventual moral convictions, but also protects him from looking at the world in an incomplete, simpleminded fashion.

CONCLUSION

The example of lying has illustrated numerous considerations that apply to our choice of discipline. We must take into account a child's developmental level, the child's motives, fears, and other "hidden agenda," and even what kinds of previous parental instruction might have inadvertently contributed to the child's faulty judgment.

My main point is this: If our main parenting thrust is to provide reward or punishment for children's behaviors, we can become locked into an "antecedent-consequence" mind-set. We categorize behaviors as good or bad, and when we see them appear, we deliver the appropriate consequences. This system is very neat and orderly and relatively simple. But antecedent-consequence thinking alone does *not* take into account everything that matters. The appearance of the "bad" behavior of lying does not necessarily mean that punishment is due, yet this is what can easily happen if we are locked into an antecedent-consequence frame of reference. Stepping back a little from coercion methods could prevent this from happening: It would assist us in accounting for all relevant issues, and protect us from treating our children unfairly.

EXERCISES

1. For the following situations, choose a reaction to fit the type of lie. If it is a lie that requires punishment, pick one appropriate for the original wrongdoing, then increase it as a penalty for the lie. For examples of appropriate reactions, see page 139.

   a. Billy left his toys all over the front lawn. When asked about them, he said that Danny put them there.

   b. Joan spent her afternoon playing with her friends, and as a result did not have time to get her homework done. When her teacher informed Joan's parents, Joan said she had forgotten to bring it home.

   c. Mary climbed onto the counter and knocked the forbidden cookie jar onto the floor, breaking it into many pieces. When her mother asked her about it, she said she didn't know how it happened.

   d. David brought his dog into his room overnight instead of putting him outside, as he had been instructed. During the night the dog had an intestinal ailment and left its evidence all over the living-room carpet. When asked about it, David said someone must have let the dog back in after he let him out.

   e. Jimmy accidentally stepped on his baby sister's fingers. When asked why his sister was wailing, he said he didn't know.

   f. Four-year-old Jeffy comes running into the house saying Mickey Mouse visited him while he was playing in the front yard.

2. For the following spiritual guidelines, explain in writing *why* God gave us such instructions. See pages 139–40 for sample explanations.
   a. Love thy neighbor.
   b. Obey the law of the land.
   c. Forgive one another.

CHAPTER NINE

Picking Up the Pieces

In this book we have discussed a number of ideas that can improve our ability to encourage our children's moral growth. A part of looking at these ideas has included challenging some of the old standard beliefs concerning building morals. We have seen how the punitiveness involved in coercion models of discipline can actually work against moral development. We have explored how demanding absolute, unquestioning obedience results in adults who have little internalized conception of right and wrong. We have mentioned the importance of allowing children to express their anger over the disciplines imposed on them, and that it is not disrespectful of them to do so.

Now that we have cast some doubt on past notions, how do we proceed? How can we teach our children to respect us without demanding absolute obedience? And what about consistency? Children find security in knowing where their boundaries are. If we want to let them negotiate what we ask of them, how can they know they have boundaries?

What about the absolutes involved in religious teachings? Scripture makes frequent reference to the use of the rod in discipline. How can Christian parents be true to their faith if they do not heed the literal interpretation of the "rod" passages?

We will tackle these dilemmas now.

RESPECT VERSUS OBEDIENCE

There is little doubt that learning to respect authority is an important part of any child's upbringing. Most coercion models of discipline approach teaching respect with demanding absolute obedience.[1] The rationale is that once a child is taught to respect the fact that the parent will have her way, the child will also respect the parent, and in turn will be receptive to what the parent has to say about religion, morals, and so on.

I propose that this argument is not only convoluted, but also tries to approach the problem in a regressive manner. First, there is no reason to believe that teaching a child that his parents are going to have their way results in any kind of healthy respect for the parents. As Missildine so aptly put it, as quoted in chapter 5, punitive measures result in obedience, but it is a product of hateful respect. The child obeys because of respect for the power wielded by his parents, not respect for the parents themselves. Therefore, the entire premise for demanding absolute obedience as an avenue toward teaching respect and morals is highly questionable.

Second, this rationale is not addressing why we want children to respect authority. Respecting authority is a concrete rule based on moral principles. Authority is created for the purpose of promoting moral principles, such as justice, fairness, and consideration and caring for all members of a constituency. If children have been raised with these principles, respect for authority will follow, since the activities of the authoritative system are designed to support the same principles.

Obedience should be directed toward a set of moral principles, and not to some concrete figure or system. We would not want our children to proclaim undying allegiance toward the next Hitler, should one come along. However, we would want our child to cooperate with forms of authority that protect everybody's rights, care for the downtrodden, and prosecute those who harm others. The child's allegiances should therefore be directed toward what authority stands for, not toward the individuals who currently hold status within the authoritative system.

Respect for parents is important for reasons other than as a tool for coercion and teaching primitive concrete rules. Respecting parents is part of an interpersonal interaction style that goes beyond reactions to authority figures. In order to live peacefully in our society, children need to learn to respect all human beings just because they are other human beings. Through the avenue of teaching respect for parents, then, it is not their status as authority figures that is most important. It is the fact that they are human beings, and give the child an opportunity to practice interacting with others in a way that respects the principles of caring, consideration, and justice.

Schulman and Mekler make this important point about the relationship between respect and obedience:

> Keep in mind that the opposite of an oppositional child is not an obedient one. It is a respectful and cooperative one. If your youngster respects you, she will *give* you authority over her. You won't have to drag it out of her. On the other hand, if you demand unquestioning obedience from her, the only way to get it is by making sure she fears you and has no confidence in herself. Cooperation is a two-way street.[2]

We have already looked at some ways we can encourage respect for others' rights and feelings. Moral exhortation, reasoning, and explaining motives all show how to connect our inner principles with outward behaviors. Schulman and Mekler emphasize the importance role-modeling plays in teaching respect. They make four main points.[3]

1. "Recognize that his activities and interests are truly important to him." Although some childish pastimes may seem pretty unimportant to us, children have a different viewpoint. They see their activities as being every bit as important as ours. If we laugh at their interests, we are telling them that we do not respect their feelings. Likewise, if we interrupt them in the middle of something they are really enjoying in order to make them do something we consider more important, we are again saying that we don't care about what they find to be personally satisfying. What this does is to model the lesson that others' feelings don't matter, and children are likely to act toward others in the same insensitive way.

This type of modeling is prevalent in homes where coercion is the primary mode of discipline. For example, a child has been working on a building block project all evening. Bedtime approaches. His mother says, "Time for bed. Get going!" "Just a minute," the child replies, as he carefully balances the finishing touches on his masterpiece. Since his reaction to her demand did not consist of absolute, immediate obedience, she delivers the consequence of whacking him on the behind or some other form of pain. The child's feelings and aspirations are therefore ignored, if not veritably degraded.

Schulman and Mekler point out that if children are cautioned ahead of time that there will be a time limit on their activities, there will be less complaining and hassle when the activity must end. This notion has been supported by research,[4] and certainly models a more humane way of treating another human being.

2. "Recognize and respect your child's style of loving." Different children show affection in different ways, and we can model respect for others by allowing them to define what feels comfortable for them. Some children like lots of hugs and kisses, and others prefer pats on the back accompanied by kind words. If we want more affection than our child is giving, there is nothing wrong with asking for it, but we should respect our child's right to say that we are asking for more than he can feel comfortable with.

3. "Recognize that she has a right to her own tastes and preferences." Nothing is more flattering than to have another person imitate us in our mannerisms or preferences. Unfortunately, parents often expect their child to take on their preferences, "follow in their footsteps," and so forth, just because the child is their own. Forcing children to define themselves in a way that satisfies our own desires is self-centered and insensitive. It shows the child that we do not respect who he is or what he is interested in. It also increases the probability that he will demonstrate the same insensitivity toward others.

Allowing a child to state preferences that are not the same as his parents' is not disrespectful. What difference does it make if a child prefers chicken to pork chops, or would rather be on the soccer team than play in the band? Give children choices whenever it is appropriate. By encouraging them to assert their preferences, we both build their self-confidence and provide a model of supporting and cooperating with others' desires.

4. "Recognize and respect the fact that your young child must first be taught the rules of 'good' behavior before he or she can be expected to follow them." Most of this book has been devoted to this concept. Teach children the principles behind good behavior, and you won't need to coerce them into obeying a constant stream of commands.

The bottom line to teaching respect is treating children like other human beings, rather than like wild animals to be controlled, manipulated, and punished. All of the above points illustrate how we would like to be treated ourselves. How do we feel when we are around those who always demand that things be done their way? We certainly don't feel particularly charitable or cooperative, nor would we pick out such a person as someone we would like to emulate. Children learn to respect us and emulate us because we act in a way that respects them and cooperates with them.

CONSISTENCY

One of the advantages of using a purely coercive model of discipline is that the child knows exactly where his boundaries are. Since he receives a consequence of some sort every time he crosses the line, boundaries are extremely easy to define. Children find security in having boundaries because they know exactly what to expect, even if what they can expect is a harsh and oppressive coercive model of discipline.

We all feel more secure with the familiar than with the new. One of the biggest obstacles in the way of change during psychotherapy is the comfort people find in the familiar. Battered spouses, alcoholics, and people enduring all sorts of psychic pain will avoid approaching life in a healthier way just because the old way is so dependable. Knowing what to expect is a strong component indeed in how we find security, and should be taken into account in our childrearing techniques.

If we are not going to demand that children deliver absolute obedience, and are going to allow them to question us, boundaries are not as easily established. Yet, children still need these boundaries in order to feel secure. Our next task, then, is to explore how to create this illusion of boundaries in a way that lets the child know that his parents aren't wishy-washy when they allow negotiation.

This task is not so difficult as it looks. The answer to the dilemma lies in making it clear when negotiation is possible, and when it is not. In order for this to work, the parent must first have clear in her own mind just what is negotiable and what is not. This brings us back to the issue of when to use a coercive intervention, and when to use a moral intervention. If you are in an urgent situation which must be controlled, negotiation is not an option. Urgency implies that there is no time for or benefit in standing around and talking about it.

But if you really think, most of the time when we are trying to get our child to do something, the situation is not urgent. For example, if we tell our child to pick up his toys, and he says he would prefer to wait until "Sesame Street" is over before complying, is that really such a big deal that it cannot be negotiated? Or if a child hasn't completed his homework and wants to play with his friends during the limited daylight hours of winter, is it really so terrible to allow him to wait until after dark to finish his school work? Negotiating nonurgent requests teaches the child that we are both approachable and reasonable, and encourages him to be likewise. Furthermore, negotiation helps the child see *why* things are done a certain way, so he will be able to make similar judgments in similar situations in the future.

Establishing with your child when negotiation is possible and when it is not can be accomplished a number of ways. How you choose to do it is going to depend a lot on your own personality, the personality of your child, and your family's style of interacting. The ways I am about to suggest are only options; you may find other ways of drawing these lines that work best for your family.

The first possibility is in how you phrase your request. If the issue is nonnegotiable, phrase it as a command; if it is negotiable, put it in the form of a question. For example, "Would you please pass the potatoes?" lets the child know that he can negotiate to wait a few seconds or defer to someone else if he needs to finish

buttering his roll first. Saying "Move the potatoes!" because
they are sitting on the edge of the table and are about to be
knocked off has a lesser sense of negotiation to it.

The question-command distinction is particularly good because we can clearly explain to our children that this is how we
operate. Even very young children can understand the
difference between a command and a request. When our child
inevitably tests the limits of a command, we need only state that
it was a command, not a request, and that consequences will be
delivered for noncompliance.

Another means for communicating what is negotiable and what
is not is through our tone of voice. A tone of urgency and louder
volume both show that the issue cannot be questioned at the time
of the command. At other times our more relaxed expressions of
instructions or requests show that we are open to question. Our
children can learn that under these circumstances, they are free
to ask about the orders they are receiving. It could turn out that
once the purpose of the request is made clear, they will not find it
to be so objectionable. Likewise, we could find out that we do not
have all of the facts, and that we may want to change or cancel
our requests.

Although relying on tone of voice to provide boundaries is a
little murkier than phraseology, children are actually keenly
sensitive to tone of voice. Children are actively seeking the rules
of their environment and are pretty good at picking up on
anything that suggests when a parent can or cannot be
negotiated with.

Another way of implying that negotiation is not possible is to
tack on a key word at the end of a command, which qualifies it as
an unquestionable imperative. Examples include "now,"
"pronto," "stat," "right now," and so on. Be creative! If your
family is going to make use of this system, brainstorm a word to
indicate "nonnegotiable" that everybody likes. Even nonsense
words like "aardvark" and "hockey puck" may be employed, if
they fit in with your family's style.

One problem that is closely tied with the negotiation issue is
back talk. A certain amount of back talk can be expected from any
healthy child, since it is a part of establishing the separateness of

his identity. He uses back talk as a means of devaluing his parents, in order to make breaking away from them less traumatic. Coercive models of discipline set the stage for an increased amount of back talk, because it comes to take the place of negotiation. Since coercion models do not provide opportunity to negotiate, children become angry and frustrated, and use the familiar outlet of mouthing off to deal with their feelings of impotence and helplessness. The coercive model deals with back talk with even more punitive measures, which results in even more frustration, and eventually even more back talk.

I propose that the most efficient way to deal with back talk is to deal with its source and its real-world implications. We first need to clarify why the child is mouthing off. Is he just feeling his oats and needing to establish his separateness? Or is he reacting to overcoercion? If we look back at recent events and see that he has been given little if any opportunity to negotiate some control over his life, the solution is simple. Leave the poor kid a little slack!

In addition to giving the child some appropriate control, he needs to know how his back talk affects others. The truth is, no matter who it is that talks to us in a smart-aleck manner, we don't particularly feel like having much to do with that person. And we certainly don't feel like negotiating any difference of opinions. We mostly just feel angry, disgusted, or perhaps even hurt.

If a child is mouthing off, the best intervention is to point out how his behavior affects you. You can then ask the child what he hopes to accomplish by speaking that way, and if he can tell you, you can help him find alternative means for meeting his need. If he is not aware of why he is mouthing off, you could try commenting, "Well, you sound really angry. Could you try repeating that in a calmer voice?" If he has grown up under the coercive model, he may not know how to go about assertively expressing his needs and desires. Back-talk interventions provide the perfect opportunity for teaching children how to state simply what they would like or what they believe, without acting counterproductively obnoxious.

It is important that children know they are the losers when they use back talk, that they know it will not get them what they

want. We would not bother to try to negotiate with one of our
peers if he or she were acting obnoxious and unreasonable. Why
should we encourage our children to believe that we would do
differently with them? (Likewise, we need to be aware of when
we are being obnoxious and unreasonable with them!) If we go
ahead and negotiate while they are being obnoxious, they learn
that if they mouth off, they may get their way. So, if they won't
talk civilly, don't proceed with negotiations, and tell them why.
Once they express their desires in a socialized way, then
consider their preferred options, and be sure to let them know
how much you appreciate their changed attitude.

There are times, as we all know, when if we give our child an
inch, he will try to take a mile. Instead of accepting our rational
explanations for why he is going to have to do something our way
after all, he will continue to ask "but why?" perhaps as a stalling
tactic. This can turn into a real circus if you feel as if you have to
come up with yet another reason every time your child asks for
one. If you've already given an adequate, understandable
explanation, tell him the subject is closed. Unless he has a new,
legitimate angle to explore, the topic should no longer be open
for discussion.

Of course, "Because I said so" is not an adequate rationale.
What it tells our child is that we either don't feel like answering
him, that we are inflexible, or that we are not trying to be
reasonable. It conveys the same message as ordering a child to
do something without any explanation at all: "Forget about right
and wrong, ignore your feelings, clam up, and obey!"

The explanation should include the real reasons we are asking
him to do something. We tell him to put things away after he uses
them so that others can find them when they want them. He is
required to keep the junk cleared off his bedroom floor because it
creates an obstacle course that could result in people injuring
themselves. We do not let him eat snacks just before dinner
because snacks interfere with having an appetite for the
nutritious foods served at dinner. Giving a child reasons why
various rules exist gives him a framework for developing how he
will decide right and wrong once he starts designing his own rules
and values.

If we cannot think of a reason we have set up a certain rule, perhaps we should question why the rule exists. Could it actually be something set up for our own selfish convenience? We do need some rules that take into account our own needs, such as requesting that we not be disturbed while doing something important or potentially dangerous. But what about a less important need, like not being disturbed while watching television? Is this a right that we can reasonably demand? And what about demanding that children not act like the normal rambunctious critters they are? Could it be that sometimes we set up our children for inevitable punishment when we tell them to "settle down," when by nature they cannot?

Once when I was visiting the home of one of Bridie's friends, the children were playing "ghostbusters" in the playroom while the mothers were socializing in the dining room. Bridie's friend's mother decided that the noise was getting too loud, and told them to play more quietly. They made a valiant attempt to follow her instructions. However, there is absolutely no way that young children can play a run-and-chase game without letting out a few yelps and hollers. In a few minutes, the mother tracked them down and delivered the consequence for misbehavior, which in this case involved confiscating the "ghost"—the cherished eighteen-month-old brother of one of the girls.

In my opinion, these kids were set up to be punished. There is no way a bunch of preschoolers could have figured out that the mother's request was not possible, and that a change of game was necessary before the noise could end. The mother could have ended the noise by showing the children how to play house or school with the toddler, which would reduce the noise without setting them up for punishment.

Here is another example of how being locked into an antecedent-consequence mind-set can result in children being treated unfairly. At times we may need to focus more on how we control our child's situation, rather than controlling the child. If a child cannot sit still through something, if he has reached his "sitting still" threshhold, we can take him someplace where he can run around. If he can't play a certain game in the house without an undue amount of running, we can help organize a different game or have him take the game outside. If he has difficulty playing with a certain toy without causing problems, we can find him a different toy. But we cannot demand that he conform to our wishes, when experience has shown us that our desires are beyond his abilities. That would be a set-up.

ALLOWING THE EXPRESSION OF EMOTIONS

We have lightly touched on the importance of allowing children to express how they feel. Chapter 1 pointed out that the childhood training of the Third Reich leaders had interpreted the expressions of negative feelings toward adults as disrespectful; hence, they permanently turned off their feelings and their adult crimes resulted. Chapter 3 discussed the necessity of being in touch with our feelings before we can be altruistic. Yet we are often uncomfortable about letting our children express their hurt, anger, or frustration concerning the discipline we use with them.

A good deal of our hesitance can be traced to how we view the expression of anger in general. Chapter 6 discussed how we may have a tendency to see anger as being the same as aggression. If we perceive our children's angry feelings as aggression, anger would indeed be disrespectful. Aggression toward parents is unacceptable. However, if we learn the lesson that assertive self-expression is something at which we need not take offense, we can learn to respect our children's feelings. Once they realize that we are not going to thwart their healthy emotional responses, we can assist them in learning to express emotions assertively, rather than passively or aggressively.

Alice Miller discusses at least two other important reasons children need to express negative feelings.[5] One is the avoidance of neurosis. She points out that parents can make numerous childrearing blunders yet still turn out a reasonably well-adjusted child, as long as the child has been allowed to express his anger or hurt concerning how he has been treated. It is not typically the unfairness of poor discipline that messes kids up; it is the buried feelings they are not allowed to express that leads to problems.

The second reason is that dispelling anger is necessary for

forgiveness. We can usually muster forgiveness cognitively. "Forgiveness is supposed to be healthy; therefore, I will forgive this person for what he has done to me." However, emotionally, forgiveness may not have taken place. If we do not express or openly deal with the emotional impact of the transgression, our feelings will not comply with the dictates of forgiveness. When this has happened, we may find that in spite of our claim to have forgiven the person, we still have vengeful or hurt feelings toward him concerning his misdeed.

Eventually we store up so many of these emotional wounds that the bleeding interferes with our lives. We may drive ourselves toward trivial perfection, never being satisfied with our accomplishments; or find ourselves desperately seeking the love and approval of everybody, never satiating our starved need for closeness. Another possible outlet would be various indirect "getting even" tactics, such as those of the passive-aggressives described in chapter 6. All of these outlets are indicators that forgiveness has not taken place emotionally.

As we saw in chapter 6, assertive expression of emotions allows us to say how we feel without treading on the feelings of others. For example, if our child were angry about having to go to bed early on a school night, an aggressive response would be to yell obscenities at his parents, break objects, or call his parents a couple of "jerks" (or whatever other "out-word" is his favorite at the time). An assertive emotional response would be to angrily say, "Boy I'm angry about this. I really wanted to stay up and see that new television program. You may say this is fair but it sure doesn't feel fair." He might even start crying, which is another healthy outlet for hurt or anger. The parents would sympathize with his feelings, saying they understand how he feels and they're sorry he feels bad about it. However, since no adequate excuse has arisen for staying up late on a school night, bedtime must still stand. Through this type of parent-child interchange, the child learns that although his parents won't give him everything he wants, at least they love him and support his feelings, and his feelings are O.K.

WHAT ABOUT SCRIPTURAL ABSOLUTES?

The most salient question for Christian parents is how to lessen their grip on the rod when so many scriptural passages seem to promote the tightening of that grip:

> He who spares the rod hates his son, but he who loves him is careful to discipline him. (Prov. 13:24 NIV)

> Folly is bound up in the heart of a child, but the rod of discipline will drive it far from him. (Prov. 22:15 NIV)

> Do not withhold discipline from a child; if you punish him with the rod, he will not die. Punish him with the rod and save his soul from death. (Prov. 23:13-14 NIV)

Jesus' favorite means of getting a point across was through parables. We find that the Old Testament is also filled with spiritual lessons taught through analogies. The psalms are particularly rich with them. For example, "The Lord is my rock, my fortress and my deliverer; my God is my rock, in whom I take refuge" (Ps. 18:2 NIV). God is not actually a piece of stone. The psalmist was not suggesting that we find ourselves some boulder to worship. He was describing the strength and protection of God the best way he knew how, which meant comparing him to a rock.

The psalms also speak figuratively of the rod. Ironically, the best known of all the psalms mentions the rod. "The Lord is my shepherd, I shall not be in want. . . . your rod and your staff, they comfort me" (Ps. 23:1, 4*b* NIV). The psalmist did not mean to say that God actually has a stick in his hand, that when we err he clobbers us over the head with it, and boy do we enjoy it! The psalmist was simply comparing the comfort we experience as a result of God's discipline to that of a sheep as it is guided back into the flock by the shepherd's rod. Personally, I tend to experience God's chastisements more as an inner "twang" than as a cranial blow. At any rate, we can see that in this passage, the rod represents admonishment in general, rather than an actual rap on the noggin. Could it be that the other "rod" segments are speaking figuratively as well?

Additional clues can be found within the passages themselves. For example, "If you punish him with the rod, he will not die" is an obvious falsehood if taken literally. Child protection agencies across the continent can attest to the fact that children can be beaten to death with a rod, and that it occurs with some regularity. If Scripture is to be accepted as true, our literal interpretation of this verse must be what is off. The writer is probably telling us that discipline will not destroy our children, and is using the term *rod* because of its familiarity to the sheepherding culture of the day.

Another interesting observation is that the use of the term *rod* as an instrument of discipline is used frequently in the Old Testament, but only in two instances in the New Testament. One usage is found in Revelation, which is in essence the final parable. The other usage is found in I Corinthians 4:21, where Paul writes, "Shall I come unto you with a rod, or in love, and in the spirit of meekness?" (KJV).

The New Testament introduced the overriding importance of the principle of love. Jesus instructed that love is the principle behind the law, and that it must be considered above all else. And now we find in the I Corinthians passage that the actual use of a rod is exclusive of love. Using the word *or* means we cannot have it both ways. The verse tells us that we can come to a person with a rod, *or* we can come to a person with love; but the two do not coexist. In view of this passage, how can we simultaneously accept the commandment to love and still strike children with objects?

The disciples once asked Jesus why he spoke to the people so often in parables. Here is part of his reply: "The knowledge of the secrets of the kingdom of heaven has been given to you, but not to them. . . . This is why I speak to them in parables: Though seeing, they do not see; though hearing, they do not hear or understand" (Matt. 13:11, 13 NIV).

Could it be that we have been the "them" who have been missing the boat? Have we been hearing these "rod" passages, yet not understanding? Have we not understood the "rod" passages to be analogies because of our own spiritual lacking? Can it be that if we really were in touch with Jesus' overriding command to love, we would have more easily seen the hypocrisy of teaching a child not to hurt others, then striking him ourselves? Considering this either-or relationship between love and violence, how can we continue to say "I spank you because I love you;" especially in view of the fact that pairing pain with love is the classic training for masochism? Could it be that our "sinful" nature, our tendency to want to strike out at others when we are angry, is the true guiding force that has led to the literal interpretation of these passages?

These questions are not ones that can be answered by me alone. The responsibility for responding to these dilemmas lies within us all. We have empirical research that backs these verses when interpreted as analogies, and contradicts them when we take them literally. All of us must search our souls and weigh all of the evidence, both scriptural and empirical, in order to find which way we believe God intended us to view these passages.

Another issue for religious parents is how to teach clearly stated scriptural absolutes. When we instruct our child that what the Bible says is correct, some caution is in order concerning how we present the material. It is easy to tell a child that he must not steal because "God tells us not to." This is in fact true. One of the reasons we do not steal is because stealing is prohibited in the Ten Commandments. But as we discussed in chapter 8, when our sole explanation for telling a child not to do something is because God tells us not to, simpleminded thinking is encouraged. In addition, an externalized attitude is formed. The child is taught to guide his behavior according to what seems to him to be an outside influence. When this externalized stance toward God is encouraged, an internalization of his values is difficult. And without internalization, the child will stray.

Stating a rule and saying that it must be followed only because God says so also implies to a child that there will be punishment for those who do not comply. This makes God look like a merciless monster who invents a bunch of rules for the sole purpose of being able to create punishments for when we fail. We know this is not true, since scripture describes God as a God of love, not spitefulness.

Our presentation of God's rules will appear less tyrannical if we focus instead on *why* he requires certain things of us. God gave us rules so we can be better able to apply his principles of love and justice. His rules assist us in feeling spiritually complete, and in helping others come to know him. His laws are the key to a happier existence while we are here on earth, and are also the key to our spiritual afterlife. God gave us the law because he loves us, and wants us to be happy.

Internalizing scriptural laws is a product of knowing what they are for. Instead of saying, "Do it because he told you to," we can explain how the rule fits into God's principles. For example, we can tell our child, "God has given us the rule that we should not steal things because it is not fair to the true owners. An owner would be sad if something rightfully his were taken away, and would be angry with the person who stole it. God wants to help us all love one another, not be angry with one another." Explaining rules in this manner equips children with the tools for applying scripture to their lives.

"Train a child in the way he should go, and when he is old he will not turn from it" (Prov. 22:6 NIV). This is a standard line used by those of us who are in a habit of blaming ourselves for our children's failures. We interpret it as meaning that if we had done a good enough job of raising our kids, they would have turned out to be perfect.

As scripture describes God, it doesn't sound as if he expects us to be perfect parents. Likewise, it doesn't seem that he expects our children to grow up to make flawlessly moral choices during their lives. God knows us. He knows that we all will fail at some point in doing what he would prefer us to do. That is why he sent a Redeemer. When we see true failure in our lives, we can confess it and ask for forgiveness. And it is our children's responsibility to confess and ask for forgiveness for their moral failures.

The possibility remains that we are not interpreting this verse correctly. When we read this verse, at first glance it would appear to be saying that if we successfully cram our child into the "way he should go" mold, he will forever hold its shape. But scripture repeatedly points out that we are all responsible for our own behavior. The entire message of salvation concerns each of us making our own choice to live transformed lives through Christ. It does not make sense that God would hold parents completely responsible for how their children choose to run their lives.

Maybe "way he should go" is not meant to describe the behaviors we force on our child. Perhaps "the way he should go" is actually what our "training up" should be like. God may be telling us that if we train in a way that is Christ-like—within his principles of love and justice—our child's internal make-up will not stray from these principles we have modeled for him. He may make errors in judgment and occasionally fail at living out these principles, but the principles of love and justice would still be an integral part of his being.

We have thoroughly investigated how to discipline in love. We do not need to rely on the coercive interventions of hitting, yelling, and forcing while trying to create morals. We will always need to make occasional use of heavy-handed tactics when our children's immature behaviors must be controlled. But we cannot kid ourselves into believing that we are also helping our children's morals when we use them. Coercive methods teach the principle of exerting power over others, not the principle of love. Reasoning, inner labeling, explaining, and providing a consistent model of loving and caring behavior all guide our children toward using the Lord's way of love.

CHAPTER 2: FEARS

1. "My children must always love me or I will be miserable."

    It would be nice if my children always loved me, but I can't realistically expect this to happen. As a parent I will often be requiring things of my children that they don't like or fully understand the necessity for, and it is only natural that they would feel upset with me. Furthermore, why should my happiness be contingent on my children loving me? It is uncomfortable when my children are upset with me, but that doesn't mean I have to be miserable because of it. My personal happiness and life satisfaction depend on *me* meeting *my* personal goals, enjoying *my* personal experiences, and guiding *my* life with *my* own personal moral standards; not on whether or not I win my children's or anybody else's love and approval.

2. "Making a childrearing mistake is terrible."

    Childrearing mistakes are unfortunate and sometimes result in unpleasant consequences, but they are a part of life. Besides, they point out opportunities for us to learn and grow as parents. If we have offended against a child through our error, we then have an opportunity to model such things as apologizing, asking forgiveness, and making restitution. Everybody makes mistakes. Are we all then "terrible" because we make mistakes? Of course not! We're all just human; none of us is perfect.

3. "My own childhood experience must always affect my parenting."

    Where is that written? Where is the proof? Psychological research suggests that having a certain type of background results in our having tendencies to feel like parenting in a certain way, but we can still choose whether or not we will actually parent in the way our immediate impulses may dictate. We aren't programmed, like machines; we are human beings, and have choices in our behaviors.

4. "Every childrearing problem has a perfect solution."

Who says? How do you know? And there are many problems where virtually any option is going to result in the parent, the child, the sibling, or some other involved party becoming disgruntled. You can't please everyone! All we can do is continue reaching into our bag of parenting tricks until we find the solution with the most adaptive results, not the perfect solution.

5. "Healthy parents don't get upset with their children."

Why not? Having emotions is a normal reaction to what is going on around us. We're built that way. If things are going well, we are more likely to feel good; if things are going poorly, we are more likely to feel bad. It is not the fact that we become upset that is unhealthy; it is how we react to our children when we are upset that can be harmful, or unhealthy.

6. "I must never show any weakness in front of my children."

Ridiculous. Everybody has weaknesses. Why teach our children to expect otherwise? They can learn from watching how we deal with our weaknesses. And if they never see our weaknesses and imperfections, they will expect to live their own lives in a flawless way. What a set-up for disappointment!

CHAPTER 4: WHAT TO DO AFTER YOUR CHILD DOES SOMETHING GOOD

1. Inner labeling

   a. "Thank you for taking out the garbage. You are a very helpful person."
   b. "You must be a generous person to have given part of your allowance to the church."
   c. "You children are so cooperative and obedient; you got in line so nicely. I like that."

    d. "I liked the way you helped Tommy; it shows that you care about other people's feelings. That's a neat way to be."

    e. "The way you're taking turns shows how cooperative and grown up you children are."

2. It may take a while to think of times when your children have spontaneously behaved altruistically, since it is a new thing to watch for. If you are having a lot of trouble thinking of examples, you may want to wait until after you have watched your child for a week or so specifically for spontaneous acts of altruism before doing this exercise.

3. Here are some examples of making offers of altruism workable. Try to design the task so that you will not have to do it over yourself. Doing it over after the child has done it makes him feel his help was really not worth the effort.

    a. Help fold the laundry: Allow them to do whatever their skill level will allow. Very young children can be allowed to fold towels or stack underwear, and older children can be shown how to fold shirts and pants, and take responsibility for putting things away.

    b. Help dig weeds: The big concern here is the difficulty the child may have distinguishing between weeds and plants, which could result in barren flower beds. This can be avoided by instructing the child to pull only one specific type of weed, such as grass plants. Very young children can be told to pick all of the dandelions, as long as there are not any other small, yellow flowers in the garden that can be confused with them.

    c. Bake cookies: A young child on his own in the kitchen has the potential to create a disaster area. This can be controlled by giving the child specific tasks in cookie making: fetching things from the drawers or refrigerator, adding parent-measured ingredients to the bowl, or helping stir—if the parent has used a big enough bowl to ensure that slopping over the edges will not be a problem. Older children can be shown how to shape the cookies. It is not important that they turn out perfectly; let children enjoy their accomplishment!

    d. Help take out the garbage: An older child can do this on his own. A younger child can help by carrying out larger single trash items such as milk cartons, taking the lid off the garbage can and putting it on again for the parent, separating out aluminum cans for the recycler, or perhaps carrying in the empty trash container or fetching a new trash container liner or trash bag.

CHAPTER 5: WHAT TO DO AFTER YOUR CHILD MORALLY OFFENDS

1. Moral exhortations

    a. "Oh, Sarah. Tanya must be so sad that she can't have a turn on the tricycle. That's why we always try to take turns and share our things."

    b. "It's too bad you aren't helping, Timmy. Jimmy wants to play in the sandbox too, but he can't while he's still carrying toys out. It's nice when we can help out people so they can have fun too."

    c. "Dick and Jane had to sit there and feel hungry while you were late. If you had done what you were told this would not have happened. It is a good idea to cooperate."

    d. "Jenny is so sad that you took her crayon. Now she doesn't have one. It is best to ask if you can use things, not just take them away."

    e. "It would have been nice if you had stayed and helped Lucy. Her knee hurt and she was crying. It is nice to help people when they are hurting."

2. "Ask-don't-tell" responses[1]:

    a. "How do I feel about that kind of language around the house?"

    b. "Are you cooperating?"

    c. "What are the effects of your whining and complaining on the rest of the family?"

    d. "What should you do after you've hurt someone?"

e. "How can you solve this problem?"

f. "When you make demands instead of asking nicely, how do I feel?"

g. "How can you be helpful in this situation?"

CHAPTER 6: MODELING AND EMPATHY TRAINING

3. Explaining motives

   a. "I'm glad I helped that blind man get across the street. He could have been hit by a car very easily, since he can't see where he is going. I feel better knowing that he is safe now."

   b. "She was so unhappy and her knee hurt so bad. I feel good that I was able to help her feel better."

   c. "He must be feeling really worn out taking care of the family all by himself and having to work too. I'm glad I made it a little easier for him by fixing part of their dinner."

4. Empathic monologues

   a. (*Star Wars* figures) "Uh oh. Here comes Darth Vader with his light saber. He's trying to capture Han Solo. He's scared. Here comes Luke Skywalker! He has his light saber too. He's chasing away Darth Vader. Han Solo is safe now. Luke is glad that his friend is safe."

   b. (dog and cat puppets) "The cat has all the blocks and the dog doesn't have any. The dog is so sad; he would like to have some blocks to play with too. Look, the cat is giving some of his blocks to the dog. The dog and cat are happy now. They are having such a good time stacking blocks together."

   c. (dolls) "Betsy Wetsy just dropped her cup on the floor and spilled her tea all over her new dress. She doesn't like having her dress all wet, and now she doesn't have any tea, either. She's sad. Barbie will help her. She is drying off Betsy's dress and pouring her some more tea. There, Betsy, isn't that better?"

CHAPTER 8: LYING

1. Punishments for lying

   a. Billy cannot take his toys outside for one day for leaving them out; a second day for lying about it.

   b. Joan does not get to play with her friends for one day for neglecting her homework; a second day for lying about it.

   c. Mary gets no cookies for one day for getting into the cookie jar without permission; a second day for lying about it. No punishment is included for breaking the cookie jar, since that part was accidental.

   d. David has to clean up the mess on the carpet for not letting the dog out; for lying about it, he has "yard duty" for one week longer than his usual turn.

   e. Since this is an accident, Jimmy is not punished and instead receives a moral exhortation, such as "You should have told us the truth so we would know where she is hurting and could help her. Being truthful is important in that way."

   f. This is a separation-exploration fantasy and should be treated as such. The parent might say, "Oh my goodness! What games did you play with him?"

2. Rationales for God's instructions (the type of vocabulary you use will need to vary according to the age of the child)

   a. Love thy neighbor. When you love someone, you care about that person's feelings and take into account the effect your actions have on that person. If all of us truly loved one another, we would not do things purposely to hurt one another. There would no longer be suspicion and distrust, since everyone would know that others would have everyone else's best interests at heart. Even when disagreements came up, they could be discussed and the most rational compromise decided on, since each party would know that one considered the other's viewpoint to be of equal importance. Love also leaves people free to be who they are as God made them, rather than distraught and phony because of trying to get people to love them through whatever means they believe will impress others.

b. Obey the law of the land. God established authority in order to maintain order. Order lets people know exactly where they stand. Without order, people are left to be harmed by the whims of whoever chooses to exert power over them. Order allows for the security of knowing that your rights are protected, as well as the rights of others. God desires order for us so he can give us that security.

c. Forgive one another. The anger we can feel when someone has wronged us is tremendous and very real. If left unaltered it can consume us, interfering with eating, sleeping, friendships, and other parts of daily living. Lack of forgiveness does nothing to harm the transgressor but does plenty to destroy us. God instructs us to forgive the transgression so we can let go of the anger and go on with our lives.

NOTES

CHAPTER ONE

1. A. Miller, *For Your Own Good: Hidden Cruelty in Child-rearing and the Roots of Violence* (New York: Farrar, Straus, & Giroux, 1983).
2. J. Dobson, *Dare to Discipline* (Wheaton, Ill.: Tyndale House, 1970).

CHAPTER TWO

1. J. A. Schmidt, *Do You Hear What You're Thinking?* (Wheaton, Ill.: Victor Books, 1983).
2. T. Jones and H. Schmidt, *The Fantasticks,* Twentieth Anniversary Edition (Printed in U.S.A.: Chappell and Co., Inc., 1978).
3. These examples of automatic thinking were inspired by R. McMullin and B. Casey, *Talk Sense to Yourself* (Lakewood, Col.: Creative Designs, 1975).

CHAPTER THREE

1. L. Kohlberg, "The Development of Children's Orientations Toward a Moral Order: I. Sequence in the Development of Moral Thought." *Vita Humana, 6* (1963), 11-33.
2. R. M. Liebert, R. W. Paulos, and G. S. Marmor, *Developmental Psychology,* 2nd ed. (Englewood Cliffs, N.J.: Prentice-Hall, 1977).
3. J. E. Grusec, "The Socialization of Altruism," in N. Eisenberg (ed.), *The Development of Prosocial Behavior* (New York: Academic Press, 1982).
4. A. Sagi and M. L. Hoffman, "Empathic Distress in the Newborn." *Developmental Psychology, 12* (1976), 175-76. M. L. Simner, "Newborn Response to the Cry of Another Infant," *Developmental Psychology, 5* (1971), 136-50.

CHAPTER FOUR

1. C. L. Smith, D. M. Gelfand, D. P. Hartmann, and M. E. Y. Partlow (1979), "Children's Causal Attributions Regarding Help Giving," *Child Development, 50,* 203-10 .

2. E.g., M. R. Lepper, D. Greene, and R. E. Nisbett (1973), "Undermining Children's Intrinsic Interest with Extrinsic Reward: A Test of the Overjustification Hypothesis," *Journal of Personality and Social Psychology, 28,* 129-37.

3. I. J. Toner, L. P. Moore, and B. A. Emmons (1980), "The Effect of Being Labelled on Subsequent Self Control in Children," *Child Development, 51,* 618-21.

4. A. M. Jenson and S. G. Moore (1977), "The Effect of Attribute Statements on Cooperativeness and Competitiveness in School-age Boys," *Child Development, 48,* 305-7.

5. R. A. Dienstbier, D. Hillman, J. Lehnhoff, J. Hillman, and M. C. Valkenaare (1975), "An Emotion-Attribute Approach to Moral Behavior: Interfacing Cognitive and Avoidance Theories of Moral Development," *Psychological Review, 82,* 299-315.

6. J. E. Grusec and E. Redler (1980), "Attribution, Reinforcement and Altruism," *Developmental Psychology, 16,* 525-34.

7. J. E. Grusec, L. Kyczynski, J. P. Rushton, and Z. Simutis (1978), "Modeling, Direct Instruction, and Attributions: Effects on Altruism," *Developmental Psychology, 14,* 51-57.

8. H. L. Rheingold (1982), "Little Children's Participation in the Work of Adults, a Nascent Prosocial Behavior," *Child Development, 53,* 114-25.

CHAPTER FIVE

1. M. L. Hoffman, "Moral Development," in P. H. Mussen, (ed.), *Manual of Child Psychology* (New York: Wiley, 1970).

2. K. Leman, *Making Children Mind Without Losing Yours* (Old Tappan, N.J.: Fleming H. Revell, 1984).

3. T. Lickona, *Raising Good Children* (New York: Bantam Books, 1983), 310.

4. W. H. Missildine, *Your Inner Child of the Past* (New York: Pocket Books, 1963).

5. C. Zahn-Waxler, M. Radke-Yarrow, and R. King (1979), "Child Rearing and Children's Prosocial Initiations Toward Victims of Distress," *Child Development, 50,* 319-30.

6. E. L. Dlugokinski and I. J. Firestone (1974), "Other Centeredness and Susceptibility to Charitable Appeals: Effects of Perceived Discipline," *Developmental Psychology, 10,* 21-28. M. L. Hoffman (1975), "Altruistic Behavior and the Parent-Child Relationship," *Journal of Personality and Social Psychology, 31,* 937-43.

7. Zahn-Waxler, Radke-Yarrow, and King, "Child Rearing."

8. J. E. Grusec, P. Sass-Kortsaak, and Z. M. Simutis (1978), "The Role of Example and Moral Exhortation in the Training of Altruism," *Child Development, 49,* 920-23.

9. J. H. Bryan, "You will be well advised to watch what we do instead of what we say," in D. J. DePalma and J. M. Foley (eds.), *Moral Development: Current Theory and Research* (Hillsdale, N.J.: Erlbaum, 1975).

10. Grusec, Saas-Kortsaak, Simutis, "The Role of Example," 920-23.

11. G. M. White and M. A. Burnham (1975), "Socially Cued Altruism: Effects of Modeling, Instructions and Age on Public and Private Donations," *Child Development, 45,* 559-63.

12. C. L. Smith, M. D. Leinbach, B. J. Steward, and J. M. Blackwell, "Affective Perspective-taking, Exhortations and Children's Prosocial Behavior," in D. L. Bridgeman (ed.), *The Nature of Prosocial Development* (New York: Academic Press, 1983).
13. G. M. White (1975), "Immediate and Deferred Effects of Model Observation and Guided and Unguided Rehearsal on Donating and Stealing," *Journal of Personality and Social Psychology, 21,* 139-48.
14. These examples are taken from Lickona's *Raising Good Children,* 319-21.

CHAPTER SIX

1. W. C. Crain, *Theories of Development: Concepts and Applications* (Englewood Cliffs, N.J.: Prentice-Hall, 1980).
2. M. E. Rice and J. E. Grusec (1975), "Saying and Doing: Effects of Observer Performances," *Journal of Personality and Social Psychology, 32,* 584-93.
3. E.g., A. Bandura, *Aggression: A Social Learning Analysis* (Englewood Cliffs, N. J.: Prentice-Hall, 1973).
4. A. Bandura, D. Ross, and S. A. Ross (1961), "Transmission of Aggression Through Imitation of Aggressive Models," *Journal of Abnormal and Social Psychology, 63,* 575-82.
5. R. E. Alberti and M. L. Emmons, *Your Perfect Right: A Guide to Assertive Behavior* (San Luis Obispo, Cal.: Impact Publishers, 1970).
6. Ibid., 270.
7. W. H. Missildine, *Your Inner Child of the Past* (New York: Pocket Books, 1963).
8. A. Miller, *For Your Own Good: Hidden Cruelty in Child-rearing and the Roots of Violence* (New York: Farrar, Straus, and Giroux, 1983).
9. G. Smalley, *The Key to Your Child's Heart* (Waco, Tex.: Word, 1984).
10. Ibid., 27-28.
11. E. Staub (1971), "The Use of Role-Playing and Induction in Children's Learning of Helping and Sharing Behavior," *Child Development, 42,* 805-17.
12. L. K. Friedrich and A. H. Stein (1975), "Prosocial Television and Young Children: The Effects of Verbal Labeling and Role Playing on Learning and Behavior," *Child Development, 46,* 27-38.

CHAPTER SEVEN

1. E. Erikson, *Childhood and Society,* 2nd ed. (New York: Norton, 1963).
2. J. Piaget, *The Origins of Intelligence in Children,* M. Cook (trans.) (New York: International Universities Press, 1974).
3. M. Schulman and E. Mekler, *Bringing Up a Moral Child: Teaching Your Child to Be Kind, Just and Responsible* (Reading, Mass.: Addison-Wesley, 1985).
4. G. K. Olson, *Counseling Teenagers* (Loveland, Col.: Group Books, 1984).
5. Ibid.
6. Ibid.

CHAPTER EIGHT

1. J. L. Francis, P. R. Pearson, and W. K. Kay (1983), "Are Religious Children Bigger Liars?" *Psychological Reports, 52,* 551-54.

CHAPTER NINE

1. J. Dobson, *Dare to Discipline* (Wheaton, Ill.: Tyndale House, 1970).
2. M. Schulman and E. Mekler, *Bringing Up a Moral Child: Teaching Your Child to Be Kind, Just and Responsible.* (Reading, Mass.: Addison-Wesley, 1985), 224-25.
3. Ibid., 225-30.
4. P. D. Zeece and S. J. Crase (1982), "Effects of Verbal Warning on Compliant and Transition Behavior of Preschool Children," *Journal of Psychology, 112,* 269-74.
5. A. Miller, *For Your Own Good: Hidden Cruelty in Child-rearing and the Roots of Violence* (New York: Farrar, Straus, and Giroux, 1983).

APPENDIX

1. Answers are taken from T. Lickona's *Raising Good Children* (New York: Bantam Books, 1983).